succulent style

succulent
style

A **GARDENER'S GUIDE**
TO **GROWING** AND **CRAFTING**
WITH **SUCCULENTS**

JULIA HILLIER
Succulent Artworks

yellow pear 🍐 press

CORAL GABLES

Cover Design and Art Direction: Morgane Leoni
Cover Photo: Julia Hillier
Photo Credits: Jim Bishop, San Diego horticulturist pg. 20 1st photo top row. • Mike Pyle of Mike Pyle Design pg. 28, 30 •
Fairyblooms pg. 51-55, 139 • Christy Odom of Christy Odom Photography pg. 152, 161, 170 center photo, 168 photo with little
girls, 164 wearing wrist corsage.

For permission requests, please contact the publisher at:
Mango Publishing Group
2850 S Douglas Road, 4th Floor
Coral Gables, FL 33134 USA
info@mango.bz

For special orders, quantity sales, course adoptions and corporate sales, please email the publisher at sales@mango.bz. For trade
and wholesale sales, please contact Ingram Publisher Services at customer.service@ingramcontent.com or +1.800.509.4887.

Succulent Style: A Gardener's Guide to Growing and Crafting with Succulents

Library of Congress Cataloging-in-Publication number: 2022933227
ISBN: (p) 978-1-64250-785-0, (e) 978-1-64250-786-7
BISAC category code NAT048000, NATURE / Plants / Cacti & Succulents

Printed in the United States of America

I like to call succulent gardens friendship gardens because succulents grow best when they're shared. Each cutting you take from a succulent becomes a new plant, and baby succulents will appear all around the stem to replace the one you've shared. With succulents, you always get more than you give.

—Julia Hillier

TABLE OF CONTENTS

Section I: In the Garden

Section II: Succulent Know-How

FOREWORD BY ANGELIQUE OF FAIRYBLOOMS

Julia teaches everything from the most basic care techniques to things she has learned along the way to create designs you wouldn't think possible using succulents. You don't have to be an expert to learn from one.

This is such an easy and captivating read that it's difficult to put down. Her beautiful photos will warm your heart and spark your imagination and desire to make your own creations. With her simple step-by-step guided chapters, you'll become an expert too!

Julia is an artist and creative genius who's passionate about nature and all living things. For as long as I can remember, she has been exploring and experimenting with succulents. Long before succulents became popular, she would talk with people about succulents, and they would look at her sideways and say, what's a succulent? Even then, twenty-five years ago, she taught classes on making succulent wreaths. She has helped pave the way for how people design with succulents today.

She has a way of becoming good friends with anyone she is around for more than ten minutes and loves to connect with others about succulents. It's how she learns and teaches others, and now, you will benefit from her knowledge as well. Enjoy!

AN INTRODUCTION TO SUCCULENTS

It's easy to become obsessed with succulents. Succulents come in all different colors, shapes, sizes, and textures. Like flowers, fruits, and vegetables, succulents get their beautiful colors from sunshine. With consistent sun, their colors stay fresh and vibrant.

And these incredible plants don't just grow from seeds. A succulent plant can grow from a single leaf or a cutting, which is just one of the things I cover in this book.

I like to call succulent gardens friendship gardens because succulents grow best when shared. Each cutting you share from a succulent becomes a new plant, and baby succulents will appear all around the stem, replacing the cutting you've shared. With succulents, you always get more than you give.

I run our small family succulent business with the help of my husband, Scott, and our amazing Succulent Artworks team. We love working together. Family and friendship are at the heart of our business.

Succulent Artworks began as a passion for succulents. First, I learned about growing and propagating them, then I got creative making wreaths and other succulent designs. Friends began asking me to teach classes and to buy my designs. As word got out, orders poured in. That was the start of what became our family business.

We live in Southern California, where great sunny weather and very little rain make being water-wise a way of life. It's also a climate where succulents thrive. Our area has countless succulent growers that fuel our passion. They're treasure troves of beautiful and unusual succulents. We've been collecting and propagating succulents for over two decades. I'm an artist with a little wanderlust, so our creativity and designs are influenced by a study of art, design, and world travel.

Our award-winning succulent designs have been featured at world-famous hotels, botanical gardens, and tourist attractions. Our designs have been in *Style Me Pretty Bridal Inspirations*, *Society Bride*, on FOX TV and HGTV Magazine, and in *House Beautiful*, *Pioneer Woman Magazine*, and more. Succulent Artworks is a go-to favorite for exclusive gifts for Mom, birthdays, weddings, and all special occasions.

Many friendships have begun by sharing a passion for succulents and cuttings from our garden. It's a great way to meet new friends.

I'm happy to share what I have learned about succulents. Here are a few things you will learn more about in the following pages:

There's an ever-changing world of designer succulents. It's still exciting to find succulents I've never seen. Did you know that you can create a new succulent hybrid by cross-pollinating two succulent flowers? And you can choose and register the official name for the new plant!

Beautiful planted succulent arrangements continue to grow and need only minimal care. In fact, succulent plants are quite independent; they thrive on a little neglect. They're also remarkably resilient. If life gets busy and you forget to water your succulents, drench the soil with water, and drooping leaves rehydrate as their roots soak up the welcome moisture.

There are a few essential tips to follow in taking care of succulents. I'll go into more detail later in the sections on Succulent Care and Dealing with Pests.

Most succulents love to bask in the sunlight. Not the burning summer sun at midday, but long hours of warm morning or afternoon sun, shining gently on their leaves, indoors or out.

Water succulents by drenching their soil, not by misting. Allow the soil to dry completely before you water again. If the weather is hot, dry, or windy, soil dries faster, so your succulents will need to be watered more often than if the weather is humid or cool. See the section on watering for more details.

Succulents store water in their leaves, stems, and roots. If there's a danger of frost, most succulents will need to be protected. If the water stored in their leaves freezes, the plant could die. Winter-hardy succulents are an exception.

Occasionally a little pest will want to call your succulent home. But most pests can be controlled or eliminated with everyday household products, like 70 percent isopropyl alcohol, a mixture of Dawn dish soap and water, or neem oil from the local garden center.

Read on. I'll teach you the art of fearless planting and extraordinary succulent design. It's easier than you think!

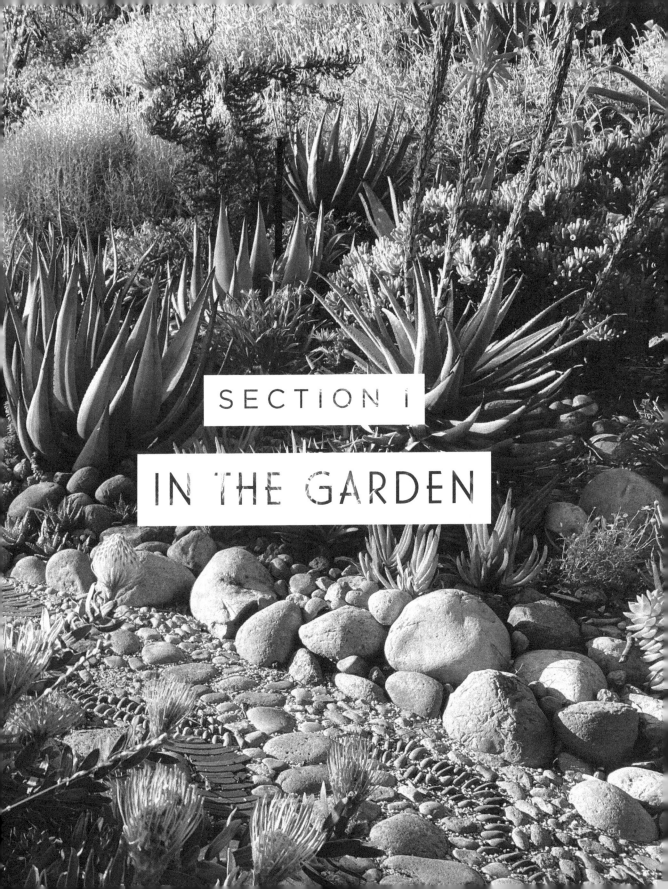

SECTION 1

IN THE GARDEN

CHAPTER ONE

DESIGN ELEMENTS

DESIGN SECRETS FROM EXTRAORDINARY SUCCULENT GARDENS

The most beautiful succulent gardens are more than a collection of succulent plants. They incorporate specific elements of design that make a garden beautiful, draw us in, and inspire!

There are several truly inspired succulent garden designers whom I have learned from, and I am excited to pass on the skills they have shared with me. Learning from them has helped me take my own succulent gardening to the next level, and I'm excited to share their wisdom.

JIM BISHOP

Jim Bishop was San Diego Horticulturist of the Year 2019, President of San Diego Horticulture Society 2011–17, and Assistant Coordinator of the San Diego Fair Flower and Garden Show 2009. His Bishop Garden Design is a six-time Garden Award winner at San Diego Fair, and he has authored sixty columns on plants for sdhortnews.org.

Jim is known for creativity, design, and his sensational succulent garden. He shared some of the design elements that have made his garden award-winning and awe-inspiring.

He begins with a plan in his mind. And as the garden takes shape and more inspiration comes, he lets the design evolve.

The garden includes cacti, drought-tolerant plants, and succulents from all over the world. And because his home is San Diego, which gets less than twelve inches of rain per year, he includes some plants that are native to Southern California.

It's important to create an entrance with a focal point that draws visitors into the garden. Then add entrances and exits throughout the garden to transition from one area to the next and invite visitors in.

An entrance can be as simple as grouping stunning plants or adding matching potted plants on either side of the entrance. Or designing two groupings of potted plants, with slight variations, one for each side.

When arranging a collection of potted plants, avoid straight rows. And include some larger or higher containers behind shorter ones. If you have lots of similar-sized pots, raise some up with a few bricks, paving stones, or a pot turned upside down.

Choosing a color theme for most of your garden pots and planters is another secret of a well-designed garden. Jim chose cobalt blue, mustard yellow, and sage green as dominant colors. He also uses terra cotta for some pots if the plant spills over the edge of the pot. Other colors are only added here and there.

Most succulents grow naturally in nutrient-poor soil. Jim uses a good potting mix, then skips fertilizing potted plants. The potted plants grow slower this way and need less repotting.

His go-to potting mix is half light soil and half perlite.

Spanish moss and tillandsias (air plants) can grow on everything in temperate or subtropical climates, so be creative! Attach them to trees; add them to pots, lanterns, or crevices in a garden wall. Remember that gray tillandsias like the morning sun and green ones are shade plants.

As you design your garden, imitate nature. Most plants don't grow alone in nature. Instead, clusters of the same plant grow together. Avoid arranging plants like islands in your garden, with a single succulent here, another there. Group odd numbers of the same plant together. Planting similar-colored plants in ribbons of color creates a beautiful tapestry without looking chaotic.

Planting in clusters also helps to keep your plants healthy. Often someone asks Jim why a plant looks so much happier in his garden than theirs. The answer is usually that theirs is growing alone. Jim plants densely, with patches of "root touching" closeness, and the plants grow beautifully.

Repeating a grouping of the same plant three times in one garden area leads our attention from one grouping to the next. This is another secret to great design.

Add a larger, eye-catching plant or tree that stands out from the others to create a focal point in the garden. If it's not tall enough to be above surrounding plants, elevate it by mounding the soil in the area beneath it. Add contoured layers to your garden by putting low features in front of taller ones.

Light gray or white plants go well with everything. They create a beautiful transition between colors that don't usually look good side by side.

Succulents grow beautifully in rock gardens. Jim recommends using local rock whenever possible. Choosing stones native to your area or property will look more natural. Cluster stones together and mix some larger rocks in with smaller ones.

When creating a dry creek bed, keep in mind that water runs downhill. Avoid straight lines; add curves to your pathways and dry creek beds. Pathways should always lead away to a hidden end. Curve the ends of pathways behind a large clump of plants or bushes to create the illusion of continuing. This makes the area look bigger and adds interest.

Use your imagination when creating garden paths and borders. A simple wall or pathway can be transformed into a work of art. Jim used discarded roof tiles, pebbles, stones, bottles, even cinder blocks, to create beautiful patterns and mosaics in walkways along borders and walls throughout his garden.

Installing a Garden Path

1. Make sure the ground is level and smooth. If you want your mosaic to be level with the surrounding area, dig out enough soil to compensate for the height of the materials you've chosen.

2. Remember that you can often cut the things you're using instead of burying them. Ask your local hardware store about renting a wet saw or another tool to cut materials.

3. Lay plastic-coated chicken wire over the soil.

4. Add a fabric weed barrier on the chicken wire to keep weeds from coming through.

5. As you lay out your mosaic design, fill the spaces with decomposed granite (DG). The DG allows water to pass through, and the mosaic can be pulled up for repairs if need be. The fabric weed barrier stops the DG from working down into the soil.

Soil was removed to allow the mosaic to be level with the pathway

Pebbles fill in the mosaic pattern

Roof tiles cut with the tile saw to create pattern

Fabric weed barrier allows water to drain, keeps weeds out of the DG from mixing with the soil

Set design in decomposed granite (DG), also use it like grout to fill small sapce

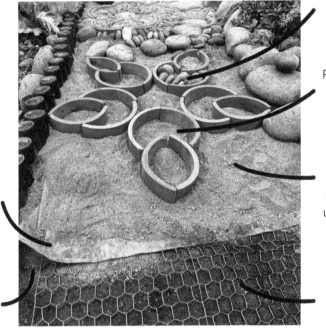

Compacted soil is smooth and level

Green plastic coated chicken wire

Gardening is trial and error. Enjoy the process—don't stress if a particular plant dies or doesn't do well in your garden. Just replace it with another plant you've been wanting.

MIKE PYLE

Mike Pyle is an American landscape designer and consultant. He is cohost of HGTV's *Inside Out*. Mike has worked in the landscape industry and been exposed to every aspect of landscape installation and design for over nineteen years.

Mike creates landscapes designed for elegant outdoor living that need minimal care. He understands the importance of relaxing in a wonderful outdoor space designed for leisure and convenience. Mike has a knack for creating the look and feel of a resort escape, even in a backyard. He generously shared some of his secrets to help you create this atmosphere in your own space.

Mike's designs are inviting. They welcome you and draw you in. The secret, he says, is in creating little moments. Areas where people want to gather, walkways where you'll want to stroll. Every square foot of a garden created by Mike is beautiful and designed for living.

Every wall in Mike's designs has a purpose. They become vertical elements with texture and contrast that draw the eye upward. He believes that walls can expand a space, rather than close it in.

Instead of the patio or walkway extending to the house's outer wall, build an above-ground planter, or arrange pots to soften the wall. An in-ground planter can be added by having an area of the concrete saw-cut and removed.

The idea is to add something to complement each wall and give it a purpose. The back of a garage can become a well-designed space for gathering around a BBQ, or a beautiful backdrop for a sitting area.

Mike even works magic with small patio gardens. He's learned secrets that maximize every square foot for outdoor living. Adding built-in benches to a table adds texture and contrast and saves two feet over chairs moved to and from the table.

Staggering stepping-stones gives pathways a more casual feel. Dymondia, a hardy succulent ground cover, looks beautiful planted between stepping-stones. It naturally flows a bit over the edges of rock or concrete but won't get crazy, so it's low-maintenance.

Notice how the succulents are planted in little clusters or families along the pathway. It looks natural, and plants grow better together, touching or almost touching.

One key to getting the feel Mike creates is keeping the plant palette simple. "Don't do twenty different succulents in an area. Instead, home in on five and repeat them in nice solid groupings."

Mike leaves spaces between clusters of plants that he often fills with decomposed granite (low-maintenance). Notice the little pockets of larger pebbles near the path that add layering and lead your eye along the path. He chooses pebbles that contrast but go well with the home, rather than interrupting our attention. Don't be afraid to use bigger rock(s) in smaller areas to add a pop of contrast.

Keep the future in mind when you choose your plant palette. It's important to know how your garden will look over time. Mike's secret to giving new gardens that beautiful, established feel right from the start consists partly of adding decomposed granite, boulders, ground covers, and other elements, and partly of choosing dwarf varieties for 60–70 percent of his plants. Their maximum size is smaller, they need less maintenance, and they can be planted closer together without outgrowing their space.

A simple landscape design works beautifully with strong (modern) architecture. The graphite gray decomposed granite in this planter goes well with the house's color. The cacti are Euphorbia MX variegated. They have a strong line without overpowering the modern architecture of the home.

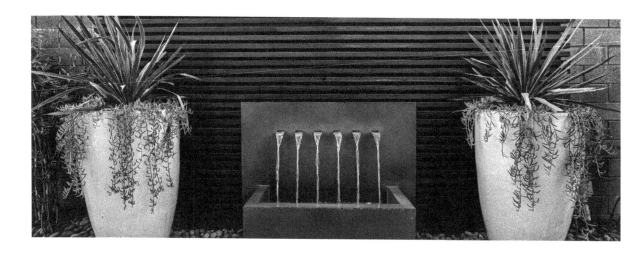

Use bold, large pots where space allows. It's better to go bigger than smaller. Large pots add a focal point to the garden. A ten-foot wall needs a thirty-six to forty-two-inch-high container. If you're using multiple pots in an area, remember that less is more. Mike usually sticks with two or three pots. If you use multiple pots in the yard, instead of mixing container colors, mix textures and use one color. Another idea is to add a pot that's a water feature.

A large area can handle a huge in-ground planter. If you have a large space for an in-ground planter, it's better to go bigger than smaller.

Mike prepares the soil for succulents by tilling and aerating the area before planting. He uses a good, premium organic cactus soil mix combined with pumice around each plant.

IDEA LIST: FAVORITE SUCCULENTS FOR LANDSCAPE DESIGN

Botanical Name/ Common Name	Height	USDA Hardiness Zone	Sunlight
Aeonium 'Blushing Beauty'	1–3 feet	9–11	coastal sun to light shade
Agave attenuata—foxtail agave	4–5 feet	6–10	sun/part shade
Agave americana—century Plant	4–6 feet	8–10	sun/part shade
Agave 'Blue Glow'	1–2 feet	8–11	sun/part shade
Agave parryi var. *truncata*—artichoke agave	3 feet	8–12	sun

Agave striata—narrow leaf century plant	1–2 feet	7–11	sun
Echeveria	8–12 inches	5, 9–12	(varies)
Graptopetalum	12 inches	7–11	sun
Hens and chicks	4–6 inches	3–8	sun/bright light
Mangaves	8–24 inches	4–9	sun/part shade
Sansevieria zeylanica—snake plant	2–3 feet	9–11	indirect light
Sedum	6–8 inches	4–11	sun/full

Xeriscape Trees	Height	USDA Hardiness Zone	Flower
Calia secundiflora—Texas mountain laurel	10–25 feet	8–10	violet
Chilopsis linearis—desert willow	15–25 feet	7–10	pink, violet, white
Prosopis glandulosa—honey mesquite	30 feet	7–11	creamy white
Jacaranda mimosifolia—jacaranda	30–40 feet	9–11	purple
Prosopis olneya var. *tesota*—desert ironwood	20–30 feet	9–11	rose to white
Olea europaea—fruitless olive	25–30 feet	9–11	creamy yellow

Ungnadia speciosa— Mexican buckeye	8–30 feet	7–10	lavender
Vitex agnus-castus— chaste, Texas lilac	10–15 feet	6–9	purple
Parkinsonia—'Desert Museum' palo verde	20–30 feet	8–11	yellow

IDEA LIST: ADDING DROUGHT-TOLERANT PLANTS TO SUCCULENT LANDSCAPES & PLANTERS

You don't have to limit your imagination when designing your succulent planter or dry garden landscape. Unleash your creativity by adding a few drought-tolerant plants or a natural element. Spark your imagination with the idea lists below.

Botanical Name/Common Name	Mature Height	Growth Pattern
Anigozanthos—kangaroo paw	1–3 or 3–10 inches	1–4 feet wide
Erigeron glaucus—seaside daisy	6–10 inches	1–2 feet wide
Festuca glauca—blue fescue	10 inches	10 inches wide
Gaillardia—blanket flower	24 inches	20 inches wide
Kniphofia—red hot poker	2–5 feet	3–6 feet wide
Lavendula—lavender	4 feet	6 feet wide
Leucadendron—conebrush	8–10 feet	6–8 feet wide or 2 feet wide

Liatris—blazing stars	3-6 feet	2 feet wide
Muhlenbergia capillaris— pink muhly grass	1-3 feet	3 feet wide
Osteospermum—African daisy	1-3 feet	1 foot wide
Pelargonium—geranium (various)	4-48 inches	3 feet wide
Penstemon centranthifolius— scarlet buglar	2-4 feet	1 foot wide
Phormium—New Zealand flax (various)	18-24 inches	18-24 inches wide
Salvia—sage (various)	1-3 feet or 3-8 feet	1-3 feet wide
Spiraea—spiria	2-4 feet	48 inches wide
*Thymus serpyllum—*creeping thyme	3 inches	spreading
Verbena canadensis— homestead purple	1 foot	3 feet wide

IDEA LIST: ADDING TOP DRESSINGS AND NATURAL ELEMENTS TO PLANTERS AND POTS

- Small driftwood accent
- Little clumps of various types of colored clumping moss
- Various natural pebbles
- Glass pebbles
- Multiple colors and textures of sand

- Long-strand sphagnum moss
- Spanish moss
- Geodes and crystals
- Wood
- Seashells
- Curly willow

MY TOOL CART

1. Stainless kitchen tongs for reaching into small spaces to retrieve or place items

2. Wire cutter, spring-loaded, electrician style, cuts thin wire

3. Flat-nosed jewelry pliers, spring-loaded, to twist and tighten wire for wreath-making

4. Metal drinking straw to tuck moss into planters and curl boutonnière wire

5. Thin leather gloves for handling cacti

6. Soft paintbrush or makeup brush for dusting soil off succulent leaves after planting

7. Wood dowels sharpened on one end have many uses: to make holes in wreaths, for planting cuttings. Blunt end to compact soil in small areas, and to press plant roots into the soil

8. Small office clamps to hold things in place after gluing

9. Wide garden trowel

10. Broken PVC pipe remover tool with small end

11. Heavy-duty scissors for cutting plants

12. Scissors for cutting ribbon and twine

13. Tin snips to cut thick wire

14. Tape measure

15. Staple gun with 9/16-inch, 14mm, T50 staples for attaching mesh to birdhouse roofs

16. Drill with a 3/8 or 1/2 inch diamond drill bit to make drainage holes in pots

MY FLORAL SUPPLIES

1.   Preserved long-strand sphagnum moss for trimming pots and mossing grapevine

2.   Hemp cord for wrapping bouquet stems and tying bows on wreaths

3.   Polyester garden mesh for wrapping moss used on birdhouses

4.   Small hemp cord for wrapping and wrapping boutonnières and bows on mini wreaths

5.   Oasis Floral Adhesive to secure small succulents in multiple designs

6.   E6000 Permanent Craft Adhesive for gluing everything but plants

7.   Weed barrier cloth for pallet gardens, and anywhere we need a soil liner

8.   Zip ties to tie grapevine wreaths together and DIY full succulent wreath forms

9.   White craft glue (I use Elmer's) diluted 50-50 with water for keeping small rocks in place

10. Floral or greening pins to secure succulents to wreaths and other designs as needed

11. Long-strand sphagnum moss, untreated

12. Large grapevine wreath for making succulent-trimmed wreaths

13. Beacon 3-in-1 Advanced Crafting glue for securing succulents if Oasis adhesive is unavailable

14. Floral wire: 22-gauge to anchor succulents to wreaths and 18-gauge for other designs

15. Floral tape: Half-inch and 1-inch for wrapping bouquets, succulent crowns, and boutonnières

16. 26-gauge floral wire on a paddle for wrapping moss on wreaths to trim with succulents

17. Snap bracelet to trim with succulents

18. Boutonnière pins

19. Craft foam board for succulent combs and slap bracelets

20. 6x3mm mini-magnets to use with mini-wreaths and other small designs for easy hanging on refrigerators and around office

21. Mini-heart and round grapevine wreath to trim with succulents

22. Kinesiology tape for succulent body art

23. Moss wreath base for succulent wreaths

24. Comb for trimming with succulents

CHAPTER TWO

INCORPORATING SUCCULENTS IN YOUR GARDEN

FAVORITE SUCCULENT GROUND COVERS

Botanical Name—Common Name

- *Dymondia margaretae*—silver carpet
- *Sedum japonicum*—Tokyo sun
- *Sedum*—'Little Missy'
- *Sedum dasyphyllum*—Corsican stonecrop, blue tears
- *Sedum spurium*—Caucasian stonecrop
- *Sedum acre*—goldmoss stonecrop
- *Sedum spathulifolium*—Cape Blanco
- *Sempervivum*—hens and chicks
- *Senecio rowleyanus*—string of pearls

SUCCULENT ROCK GARDENS

Dianne Reese is the talented designer behind Well Rooted Designs in Carlsbad, California, and has worked and designed with cacti and succulents professionally for decades. She uses her creativity and attention to detail to create beautiful succulent gardens with a calm and peaceful feeling. She's taught me elements for designing a beautiful rock garden that can transform a small patio space into a bit of paradise for relaxing and gathering with close friends.

First, Dianne prepared the space by adding soil to create a slight mound in the center. Be careful to avoid adding soil directly against a building. Mounded soil adds dimension, and helps make a small area appear larger. It's easy to do. Add a mound of soil, then smooth it with a rake into a subtle slope toward the front. Rocky landscapes are not flat. Mounded soil creates an uneven garden bed that mimics nature.

When starting a rock garden of any size, select rocks that go well with the colors in the area. The large tan rocks with rust-colored fractures that Dianne chose complement the stucco behind and the brick trim on the patio and the edge of the garden bed.

Choose several sizes of rock to create a succulent rock garden. Well-placed, large boulders or rocks provide a sense of stability. Large pebbles can add interest and help to guide the eye from one plant grouping to another. The smaller gravel or crushed rock adds texture and interest.

If you really want to include a large variety of succulents, avoid the temptation of buying too many different-colored plants. Decide on a few principal colors and stick with them. This prevents a garden from looking chaotic. Dianne chose green, yellow, and red, then added little pockets of calming lavender. Include varying heights, textures, and shapes to add interest.

Incorporate focal points in the garden, elements you can build the garden around. This can be a large or more interesting plant or rock.

Avoid planting succulents in straight rows in a rock garden. Instead, use odd numbers of the same plant, planted in staggered pockets or waves of color. This adds flow and continuity. Use repetition throughout the garden, and leave some spaces unplanted so that the eye can rest. This is a key to creating a peaceful and cohesive garden space.

Start by setting the largest rocks or boulders into place first. When placing large rocks, vary the depth by burying a third of the rock beneath the soil. This gives the look of a rock that existed before the garden rather than being set into place.

Then add the plants that will be focal points, and build out from them. Repeat patches of color three times to direct the eye through the rock garden.

Arrange big pebbles in patches or groups. Place the smaller gravel and crushed rock closest to the border of the planter. Dianne creates art in the details of the garden. Notice the interesting texture and beautiful placement of smooth stones, small pebbles, and gravel around the succulents.

The wonderful memories we create are part of the joy and charm of a beautiful garden. Resist designing a space that will create more work than you'll enjoy doing. Dianne leans toward disease-resistant plants, avoiding fussy or difficult plants that take too much coddling or pest control.

DRY CREEK BED WITH SUCCULENTS

HOW TO BUILD A DRY CREEK BED

Nature creates the most beautiful dry creek beds, so if you design your dry creek bed to imitate those in nature, you'll have a beautiful design. Dry creek or stream beds fill and flow with water seasonally with heavy rain and flooding. The path of the stream bed often follows a single meandering course with gentle curves. As you design your creek bed, avoid multiple paths and rigid lines.

Water runs downhill. Use this law of nature to help you decide the direction of your dry creekbed. If there's a slope in the yard, or you can create a slight slope in an area, let that guide the placement of the dry creekbed.

Another huge consideration when placing your dry creekbed is paying attention to where you're leading the water flow. Your dry creekbed may not always be dry, so direct water away from foundations and patios. A natural place to begin a dry creekbed is at the bottom of a rain spout, or to lead water away from areas that sometimes get flooded. If you're unsure whether there's a slight slope toward or away from something, lay down a yardstick and put a level on top to check.

As water rushes down a dry creekbed, it often carries smaller rocks and pebbles along with it. They become worn and smooth over time from water passing over them. Choosing smooth river rock and small smooth stones as the base for your creekbed will make it look more natural. Set aside stones you find as you work in your garden. What could be more natural than using rock from your own area?

Add various sizes of smooth pebbles. Larger rocks are often found along the banks of creek beds. Some large rocks and boulders along the bank can be seen jutting well into the water. These large rocks help to give a creekbed its meandering look. This is particularly helpful where there's not a lot of space to wind or bend the design of a creekbed. Large boulders or rocks below the highest level of rushing water in dry creek beds become smooth and flat, making natural stepping-stones. Adding a large flat stone to your creekbed can help you cross easily while you garden. But be sure the height is below the creek bank you've created, or it can obstruct water if the creekbed floods.

Keep in mind that nature is not symmetrical. Design with odd numbers. Three is a magic number in interior and landscape design.

Your local landscape and building supply or stone yard is an excellent place to find everything from boulders to rocks and pebbles, and it's fun to wander about. If you're looking for local rock and stone, ask the front desk, or check online to see what type of river rock is endemic to the area.

Often natural creek beds are twice as wide as they are deep. Make a three-foot-wide riverbed one and a half feet deep. Digging down and keeping the depth at that ratio, with rock in place, will look better and more natural than a flat three-foot river of rock. Use the soil from digging your creekbed to raise up the banks along the sides.

Preparing the Area: Avoid using plastic as a weed barrier. Plastic compacts soil and will prevent water from seeping into the ground. Fast-draining soil is essential for succulents, and, although the plants won't be in the creekbed, wicking water away from the plants is important. If you're concerned about weeds, consider using a weed barrier cloth.

Planting Your Dry Creekbed

Trees grow naturally beside streams and creeks. A desert tree (see the idea list on page 32) can give some shade to the yard and looks beautiful beside a dry creekbed. Don't worry about leaves that may fall into the dry creekbed. A landscape blower will clear them out easily.

The raised banks of the dry creekbed create natural drainage for succulents. Be sure to pay close attention to amending the soil and using well-draining soil in and around the areas you'll be planting.

Vary the sizes of the succulents along the creekbed, and leave some areas unplanted. Plants naturally grow in little families. Create clusters of three with rocks and with plants to mimic nature. Add plants in patches of a single color. If two patches are of different plants but have the same color, it will help create harmony and guide the eye.

And above all, have fun! Enjoy the creative process, and you'll create beautiful memories to recall each time you walk along your dry creekbed.

CHAPTER THREE

CONTAINER GARDENS

LARGE CONTAINER GARDENS

Dare to think big! When choosing a large container, consider the size of the area where it will go and the impact you'd like to create. Large areas can handle big planters, so don't be shy about choosing (a) big, wonderful planter(s) to match your vision for your large space. I'll walk you through how to plant it beautifully, step by step.

LARGE CONTAINER PLANTED WITH ONE SUCCULENT

Sedum Morganianum/
Donkey's Tail

Single specimen Agave

Stressed Aloe

If you like simplicity or you're on a budget, don't worry. Containers don't need a lot of plants. Leonardo da Vinci said, "Simplicity is the ultimate sophistication." One beautiful plant may be all you need.

Measure the area: Before starting your search for the perfect container, measure the height, width, and length of the place where your large planter will go, and jot down the measurements. It can be tricky to gauge the size of containers after you get to the nursery and start looking at all the options.

Garden pots at Green Thumb Nursery,
San Marcos, CA

Selecting a Container: Outdoor planters need a drainage hole in the bottom. If you've chosen one that doesn't have drainage, you can drill a hole. Instructions can be found on page 83. If you've chosen a container that would be difficult to drill, the container should only be used indoors. Please see the care guide for planters without drainage on page 113.

Selecting Plants for Large Container Gardens

A large single succulent can be planted in a container alone, or succulents can be arranged side by side. Overcrowding succulents in a container isn't a problem. Planting succulents side by side helps to keep them from outgrowing the container and helps plants thrive. The number of plants you use helps determine your watering schedule; more plants need more water. Check in the guide at the end of this section for details on large container garden care.

Look over the idea list of succulents for large containers to see the mature size of succulents and what to expect as they grow. Each plant's height will help you know how close to the center of the planter it belongs. Succulents planted in a container will tend to adjust their growth for their space. Some succulents can overtake an area. The Idea List of plants for large containers shows what to look for and how much to buy when you're plant-shopping and designing your container.

IDEA LIST: SUCCULENTS FOR LARGE CONTAINERS

TALL SUCCULENTS:

Name	Mature Height
Euphorbia	varies by species, 1–20 feet
Sansevieria	varies, 1–3 feet or 3–8 feet
Aeonium	varies by species, 2–3 feet (some up to 5 feet)

FAVORITE LARGE SUCCULENT:

- Agave

TRAILING OR HANGING SUCCULENTS:

- *Senecio rowleyanus*—string of beads (a.k.a. string of pearls)
- *Senecio herreianus*—string of raindrops (a.k.a. string of tears)
- *Cotyledon penden*—cliff cotyledon
- *Sedum morganianum*—donkey tail
- Sedum 'Burrito'

IDEA LIST: FAVORITE PLANTS FOR SUCCULENT DESIGNS & CONTAINER GARDENS

Botanical Name/ Common Name	Height
Anacampseros rufescens	under 6 inches
Anacampseros telephiastrum 'Variegata'/'Sunrise'	under 6 inches
Cotyledon tomentosa 'Variegata'—Variegated bear's paw	7–12 inches
Crassula rupestris—baby's necklace	7–10 inches
Crassula perforata veriegata— diamond necklace	12 inches
Crassula ovata 'Hummel's Sunset' (golden jade)	2–3 feet
Crassula perforata 'Ivory Towers' or string of buttons	12 inches
Crassula rupestris	10 inches
Echeveria 'Blue Atoll'	under 6 inches

	Echeveria 'Cubic Frost'	under 6 inches
	Echeveria derenbergii—'Painted lady'	under 6 inches
	Echeveria elegans	under 6 inches
	Echeveria 'Galaxy Blue'	under 6 inches
	Echeveria lilacina	under 6 inches
	Echeveria 'Lola'	under 6 inches
	Echeveria 'Neon Breakers'	under 6 inches
	Echeveria 'Perle von Nurnberg'	under 6 inches
	Echeveria 'Violet Queen'	under 6 inches

	Echeveria 'Ramillette'—Orange glow	under 6 inches
	Echeveria subsessilis	under 6 inches
	Gasteria 'Little Warty'	under 6 inches
	Graptopetalum superbum	under 6 inches
	Graptoveria 'Bashful'	under 6 inches
	Graptoveria 'Debbie'	under 6 inches
	Graptoveria 'Opalina'	under 6 inches
	Graptosedum 'Alpenglow'	under 6 inches
	Graptosedum 'California Sunset'	6-8 inches

	Graptosedum 'Vera Higgins'	under 6 inches
	Haworthia fasciata—Zebra plant	under 6 inches
	Kalanchoe tomentosa—Chocolate soldier	6–8 inches
	Kalanchoe tomentosa—Panda plant	8–12 inches
	Kalanchoe luciae—Paddle plant or flapjacks	12 inches
	Pachyphytum oviferum—Pink moonstones	6–8 inches
	Sedeveria 'Blue Burrito'	8–12 inches
	Sedeveria 'Blue Elf'	12 inches
	Sedum adolphi—'Lime Gold'	6–8 inches

	Sedum clavatum	6–8 inches
	Sedum dasyphyllum 'Major'—Corsican stonecrop	under 6 inches
	Sedum 'Firestorm'	8 inches
	Sedum rubrotinctum 'Aurora'—Pink jelly bean	8 inches
	Sempervivum	under 6 inches
	Senecio crassissimus—Vertical leaf or dragonfly	18–24 inches
	Senecio rowleyanus—String of pearls	vine
	Senecio radicans—String of bananas	vine
	Tillandsia—Air plant	sizes vary

UNIQUE AND UNEXPECTED CONTAINERS

Seashells, large or small, can be planted with succulents.

No pot, no problem! Let's try a short creativity game. Look around and find three items nearby. Now save that list in a memo. When you finish this section, you'll know how to make at least two of those items into a succulent planter. It's lots of fun to choose a container to plant succulents in. Be creative in your foraging!

One of the most amazing things about succulents is that you can plant them in almost any container. Many can even grow on a small patch of moss. This makes your design options virtually limitless. Everyone has their own style, but don't be afraid to break away and experiment with something new.

Succulents grow naturally side by side. They're planted side by side on wreaths and in vertical gardens. They can be planted just as closely together in a container garden. The number of plants you use will help to determine the watering schedule. Be aware of the mature size of plants and their growth patterns, so you'll be able to select plants that will go together beautifully as they mature.

This repurposed light fixture was placed in a large plastic nursery pot to help keep it upright. We used long-strand sphagnum moss instead of soil because the soil would have sifted out through the holes.

We began planting in the center with our tallest plants, then designed the left side, and last, the right. The planter's size and ornate design can look busy, so we used clumps of color to make it exciting and colorful but subtle.

The edges are trimmed with the same long-strand moss used as soil. It's naturally colored, not dyed green, so it has a softer look we were after. The string of pearls is lifted, and the moss is tucked under it instead of skipping that area. The moss will give it a softer edge to lie on.

We added plants that will grow taller toward the center of the planter: blue elf, variegated elephant bush, String of Buttons. The pink jellybeans will extend down over the planter with the string of pearls.

Succulents generally grow to the size of their container, so they will stay close to this shape for a year or more with little maintenance.

Select four or five hard-bound books to use for your succulent planter. The top book should be over two inches thick. The books can be painted or left as they are. If you're leaving the books unpainted, choose books that will look nice where you'll place them.

If you decide to paint the books, remove the book jackets and use matte finish spray paint (I chose white) to cover the outside of the books. Use a paintbrush to smooth out any drips. Allow the paint to dry between coats. Red bookbinding will take more coats to hide than other colors.

Mark a rectangle on the top book and use a box cutter to cut out the rectangle area on the cover. Continue to cut the rectangle area down through all the pages to the back cover. This space will be the planting area. You may need to open the book to reach additional pages as you cut.

Brush white craft glue on the back of each book cover to glue them together in a stack. Leave the top book's cover unglued so it will open. Next, use a paintbrush to brush white craft glue into the outside edges of the pages of each book.

Open the top cover of the book and line the planting area with thick plastic. Extend the plastic about an inch and a half onto the page. Use a staple gun to staple the edges of the plastic in place and trim the excess. Last, glue the book cover down. Turn the stack of books upside down while the book cover dries in place.

A quote can be stenciled on the bindings of the books. I used stick-on, peel-off stencils and craft paint to make the quotation look like book titles. A stencil brush has a stiff, flat top. A small sponge brush also works well.

Some examples of fun planters. Photos were taken at Succulent Café San Diego.

MEDIUM AND SMALL TABLETOP GARDENS

Succulents are universally loved. They go with any style. They look as much at home planted in a stack of books with the center carved out as they do in an elegant bridal arrangement. I've flown succulent arrangements to a superyacht in the Caribbean, delivered them to college dorm rooms, and everything in between.

CONTAINER SHAPES

If you're shopping for succulent pots, look for a good-sized opening. Many nice-looking pots have narrow necks or small openings. Choosing a pot with an opening big enough for planting is important.

CONTAINER SIZE

Before you look for a planter, it's a good idea to decide where it will go—then you'll know what size and style are best. Rectangular planters fit beautifully on rectangular tables. A grouping or groupings of containers fit most tables.

If you're choosing a container for a specific succulent plant, keep in mind that a large container can steal the spotlight from a beautiful little succulent. Also, note that succulents grow best in containers that are just a bit larger than the plant or plants you've chosen.

Both shallow and deep pots work well with succulents because they don't need a lot of soil depth for their roots to develop. A container can be as shallow as two to four inches. Succulents can stay looking beautiful planted closely together in a container.

Another thing to keep in mind is that some containers can become top-heavy. Succulents store water in their leaves and have shallow roots. They can tip over easily if planted in a lightweight container with a small base. Adding something heavy in the bottom can help to keep it stable.

FINDING YOUR DESIGN STYLE

Country may be your style if you like a relaxed look and feel. Country style is inviting. Planters are often galvanized metal, or metal with patina or distressed paint. Rustic or natural wood planters have a country look.

You may like hand-glazed ceramic and reclaimed or repurposed planters. Handcrafted ceramic and earthy natural pots, terra cotta, or woven baskets are planters you're likely to choose. These are all country-style. Country finishes are natural or whitewashed, chalk paint, and distressed.

Look outside, and you'll see the colors of country style in nature. They're muted shades of blue, browns, reds, greens, shades of yellow, and every shade of white—plus plaids, stripes, and checks.

Natural top dressings can add a lot of style to a country planter. You'll find a list of natural elements and top dressings to spark your creativity on page 34.

You lean toward a modern style if you like a clean, sleek look with strong lines and neutral colors. Containers with a modern style have simple shapes and bold, straight lines. Examples are square or rectangular planters, or a large, low-profile bowl. Modern colors are crisp white, shiny, or matte black and shades of grey, metallic silver, taupe, and brown, and a pop of color.

This leaves the door wide open for choosing a container with a bold, bright color or an interesting shape or texture, like a beautifully woven basket. My favorite modern containers are large, low-profile cement or wooden bowls and rectangular planters in wood or cement.

Contemporary style is constantly changing because it's whatever is popular now. What style are you? You'll know by the style of planter you choose.

PLANTING YOUR CONTAINER

Soil: Add enough soil to your container to come about three inches below the rim before planting. This will bring the soil level to about a half-inch below the edge after the succulents are added. If the soil is lower than that, add more under the plants as you go.

Planting: There is a trick to planting succulents in medium and small containers. Take the plant out of its plastic garden pot. Remove any soil that extends beyond the sides of the plant. Succulents do well in a planter with root-touching closeness. Don't remove soil from the bottom, only the sides. I leave the bottom soil intact so the roots will be long enough to hold the plant in the pot. Skip this step if the plant has grown to the edge of its garden pot. Next, remove any soil around the stem that touches the plant's lower leaves. This helps with air circulation and keeps moist soil off of the leaves. Always remove any dead leaves around the base of succulents. They attract pests and hold moisture.

Design: Place the first succulent against an edge of the container, and tip the plant slightly over the rim. If the roots don't touch the soil when the plant is tilted, add more soil and scoot it under the roots.

Add two more plants beside the first, with root-touching closeness, and tilt them slightly over the pot's rim, the same as the first.

Next, add a succulent with multiple stalks, like jelly beans—*Sedum rubrotinctum* (I like the variegated or 'Aurora' variety shown in this photo). Other fillers I often use are string of buttons (*Crassula perforata*), Crassula diamond necklace, and *Crassula rupestris* (baby's necklace).

Once your clustered succulents are in place, add the remaining succulents and let their tops tip slightly over the planter's edge. This will leave room for them to tuck deeper into the planter and still be just a half-inch below the edge after you've trimmed the planter edge with moss.

You're ready to moss the sides of your planter. Take clumps of long-strand moss and tuck them in loosely all around the edges of the pot. Once it's all the way around the pot, a metal drinking straw works great for securing it in place. You'll see the plants tuck into the pot as you press the moss in. All the succulent leaves should be above the edge of the pot. Press the moss down with the metal straw. Keep the straw vertical, and tuck the moss into the inside edge of the pot. Be careful not to push it in horizontally toward the succulents, or it will lift the succulents out.

Tip for removing bits of soil from your succulent arrangement: We use a large fan-shaped soft makeup brush to dust away any soil that's fallen onto the leaves. It won't loosen even the most delicate succulent leaves or disturb their powdery coating (farina).

Succulents do well in containers with a drainage hole that allows excess water to drain out. If your pot doesn't have a drainage hole and one can't be added easily, be sure to adjust the amount of water you give when watering. Give less water to ensure you never overwater the plant. See page 113 to learn more about watering pots without drainage holes.

MAKING A HYPERTUFA PLANTER

RECIPE

While mixing the dry ingredients, use a face covering. Use gloves when working with cement.

Choose something to use as a mold to form your shape. The wet mix won't stick to cardboard, newspaper, plastic, or Styrofoam. These same materials can be used to line your mold to add texture to your planter. If you choose metal or another material as a mold, spray it well with oil or cooking spray to help the mix release easily after it's cured.

1. In a large tub for mixing, combine 3 parts peat moss and 3 parts perlite.
2. Break up little clumps, toss out any small sticks, and mix together well.
3. Add 2 parts Portland cement (do NOT use cement mix).
4. Mix together thoroughly.
5. Pour 2½ parts water evenly over the dry mix.
6. Add more water as needed to make it the consistency of cottage cheese.
7. If you'd like, add cement color.
8. Mix everything together well until there are no dry patches or clumps.
9. The mixture should form a solid ball that holds its shape when pressed in your hands.
10. I like the look of a bowl-shaped stone planter. So, I'll use a plastic bowl to form the mix. I'll spray the bowl well with oil to make sure it releases easily tomorrow, after the first twenty-four-hour cure time.
11. Pack the mix in or around your mold. It should be about 1½ to two inches thick. It's very important to compact the mixture against the mold. Use a wooden block or a metal can to press firmly against the edges.
12. Poke a drainage hole in the bottom, particularly if it's an outdoor planter. Then set your hypertufa aside and cover it with a plastic bag to slow-cure for twenty-four hours, or until it feels dry.
13. Remove your hypertufa planter from the inside of the bowl. If there are any imperfections, they can be carefully smoothed or brushed away now.
14. Set your hypertufa aside to cure for an additional thirty days. so it will last through weather and time. Be sure to rinse it well with water, fill it, and allow the water to drain every day for about ten days before planting it to ensure that all the lime from the cement has leached out.
15. The hypertufa is ready to plant! Cover the drainage hole with fabric weed-barrier cloth. Add succulent potting mix and your favorite succulents. Be sure to add enough soil for your plants to be within an inch of the top of the bowl for best airflow around the soil.

STYLING CACTI AND SUCCULENTS IN CLEAR GLASS CONTAINERS

TERRARIUMS

Cacti and succulents need good air circulation and fast-draining soil to grow well. Terrariums and other glass containers offer little air circulation or drainage, and glass intensifies sunlight and heat. Select small plants that need very little water and grow well in indirect sunlight or bright shade. Low water cacti, small Aloe, and Haworthia are good choices.

Dianne Reese of Well Rooted Designs has spent years perfecting the steps I'll share with you for making low-maintenance indoor gardens. They're beautiful and able to survive with succulents and cacti.

It's fun to choose plants and top dressings for a terrarium. We live near the beach, so I went beachcombing for shells, sea fans, bits of driftwood, pebbles, and sea glass for our terrarium. Next, I went to a local shell shop to see if something else would be fun to include. See what you can find in your area. Here are a few ideas to get you thinking: interesting rocks and crystals, bits of wood—even a feather, a tiny pine cone, or a beautiful marble can add interest and color. Use your imagination while you gather things! Six or seven one- or two-inch plants are enough to fill a ten-inch terrarium

You'll need a terrarium, lightweight cactus/succulent soil, and sand. The sand we used is Natural Decorative Real Sand, in beige. It's sold for use in aquariums and crafts. The amount of sand you'll need depends on your terrarium's size and shape. We used two five-pound bags in this ten-inch terrarium made by LSA International.

You'll also need a soft brush or two to sweep any little bits of soil that fall on top of the sand as you plant. A plastic tube, like those used in bakeries as wedding cake supports, and a funnel, are helpful. The tube is great for directing sand where you need it. Another helpful tool is a pair of long, narrow kitchen tongs to reach tight spaces where hands won't fit. A wooden dowel works great for moving soil around and to help compact the soil around the roots to secure the plants in place. A turntable or lazy Susan helps turn the terrarium as you plant.

Pour sand around the inside edges of the glass, and build it up on the sides to the height you'd like the soil to be. We added two inches of sand all along the inside edge of the terrarium. Be careful to avoid getting sand on the center of the glass in the bottom of the terrarium; that's where the soil will go.

Dampen the cactus/succulent soil just enough so that it holds its shape when it's pressed in the palm of your hand. A new bag of cactus/succulent soil is usually damp when it's first opened. Put a handful of soil in the center of the terrarium where there is no sand, being careful not to let any soil fall onto the sand.

Press the soil firmly with your fist to compact it. Then add more soil and compress it again, until the soil is mounded up even with the sand on the sides of the terrarium. We'll be adding more sand along the edge as we fill the terrarium with plants.

After the soil is in place and compacted, it's time to add plants.

If little bits of soil fall onto the sand, gently brush them back onto the rest of the soil with a soft brush or paintbrush.

Use a plastic tube with a funnel on top to add more sand along the edges of the terrarium, if needed, to keep the sand slightly above the height of the soil. Use the funnel to pour sand in the top of the tube, then direct the bottom of the tube where you'd like the sand to flow out.

While you're adding plants, remember to leave little spaces for your top dressings. Once the plants are in place, use the plastic tube again to direct sand to cover all of the soil.

Add the items you've collected for top dressings after all of the plants are in place. Adding a thin strip of coarser sand along the very edge of the terrarium can add texture to your design.

Care

Place your terrarium on a table where it will get only indirect sunlight. Add water once every two weeks, directly beside each plant to dampen only the roots. An infant 5-ml medicine dropper or syringe works great for adding water near the roots.

GLASS CONTAINER WITH SAND ART

Another beautiful container is a glass cube or rectangle.

Cacti need very little water, so they are good for a glass container. Leave the cacti in their garden pots and place them in the glass container. You'll need a funnel with a narrow tip, and several textures and colors of sand for your design. Sand is available at most craft stores as well as online. A soft paintbrush is important to help adjust the sand and spread it more evenly as you layer it.

Fine sand will sift down through coarser sand, so start with the finest sand in the bottom and add coarser sands above it.

Use the funnel to pour sand exactly where you'd like it. Layer different sands to add color and texture to your design. Be sure to get each layer of sand between the garden pots and along the edge of the planter. Uneven hills of layered sand look best.

Care

Water directly around each cactus, not the entire top of the arrangement. Add enough water to dampen the soil around each cactus, not to saturate.

PLANTING SUCCULENTS IN DRIFTWOOD OR GRAPEVINE LOGS

Tip for choosing a natural wood planter: I like to choose wood with natural crevices and an interesting shape for our driftwood planters. If you live near a beach or lake, it's often easy to find driftwood along the shore. Look for wood that's wide enough to drill some one-inch to two-inch holes. Succulents don't need a lot of soil depth. The size of your log determines the size of the succulents you'll plant. If you find little bits of driftwood, they're just right for planting baby succulents. If there's no water nearby, try shopping at your local nursery. Most large nurseries carry pieces of driftwood.

If you live near a vineyard, drop by and ask for old grapevine trunks that have been cut away. Usually, there's a pile to choose from, and often it's free. Grapevine trunks have a beautiful shape and often have long crevices that are perfect for planting.

That's what I've used in this photo. Older trunks have bark that can be brushed off easily. More newly cut grapevine would need to be sandblasted for the smooth look of an old trunk. If you look up sandblasting in your area, most shops can blast a piece of grapevine in a matter of minutes for a small fee if you ask.

See what natural wood you can find for a driftwood planter in your area.

Press long-strand sphagnum moss into the crevices of your driftwood planter. Sphagnum moss is used in place of soil in a driftwood planter. I'll tell you a total secret. I use the brand SuperMoss and our favorite type is called Mountain Moss. It's available at craft stores in the floral department and online.

Most plants will stay in place if the moss is pressed securely around them. I use a metal drinking straw to secure the moss. If a plant isn't staying in place, you may want to use a little dab of Oasis floral adhesive around the bottom of the plant on the leaves. Avoid getting it on the roots. Too much on the roots will weaken the plant. Floral adhesive will keep the plant in place until its roots are established.

Some cacti are spineless and easy to plant. If the cactus has spines, be sure to use gloves. I use leather riding gloves instead of bulky garden gloves. If you somehow get a cactus spine that's difficult to remove with tweezers, try soaking it in warm water. Often they fall out or become easier to remove.

It's not important to plant every inch of a grapevine or driftwood planter. It looks nice to leave unplanted areas. If you're designing a large grapevine planter, following the design tips on color shared in Chapter One: Design Elements will help you create a beautiful design. It can add interest or color to include a few natural elements in your design, besides cacti and succulents.

DESIGNING HANGING SUCCULENT PLANTERS

HANGING PLANTERS WITH MIXED SUCCULENTS

Hanging planters are the perfect place to show off your trailing succulents. Check the planter's depth to see if the soil around the plants will be enough to raise the soil to within an inch of the top edge of the hanging planter. If the hanging planter is deeper than the pots, add more soil. I start planting hanging planters of mixed succulents by adding a trailing succulent in one end first. Always plant trailing succulents on the side of the planter so they will spill over and trail down the side, not over other plants. Next, fill in plants beside the trailing succulent. Watching the color pattern of the plants you're adding will help balance the color. If you add pink on one end, add other colors near it, then add another pink, always watching to create a pattern or an even distribution of colors.

HANGING PLANTERS WITH ONE TRAILING SUCCULENT

A single trailing succulent looks beautiful in a hanging pot. Placing it near a window to get morning or late afternoon sun will help your plant thrive. A macrame hanger is fun and easy to make. You can decide how long you'd like it to be, and it can be designed for any pot size.

Follow these steps to create your own macrame plant hanger using a square knot and a half square knot. When you know the knots, they can be used alternately to create your own design with cord. This pattern is for a five- to six-inch pot and uses a medium-weight cord.

Cord can be found at craft and hobby stores. I buy Lamb's Wool Bonnie Braided Macrame Craft Cord: 100 yards, 2mm, from Hobby Lobby; a corkboard or other firm surface that will hold a pin; a wooden or metal ring; a pair of scissors; and a tape measure. Metal office clips of different colors help separate the cords into groups.

Start by cutting eight pieces of cord into twelve-foot lengths. Pull the cord through a wooden ring and stop at forty-eight inches (NOT halfway), gather the cord below the ring. Clip the top of the wooden ring to your board with a large clip to hold it securely.

Cut a separate sixteen-inch piece of cord. Lay the piece of cord flat against the strands of cord with one end just above the wooden ring. Lift the bottom end up near the other end, making a U shape, as shown.

Hold the cord to keep its U shape with the top end up by the wooden ring, as shown.

Take the bottom end of the cord and, starting just under the wooden ring, wrap it around the entire bundle of cords ten times. Wind each wrap securely but not tightly, keeping each row close to the one above it, as shown.

After wrapping the cord ten times, thread the end of the cord you've wrapped through the little loop that's left of the U made with the cord, as shown.

To secure the wrap, pull the top end of the cord near the ring. As you pull it, the little loop below the wrap will pull up under the wrapped cords and disappear, as shown.

Cut the two loose ends of the wrapped cord off with the scissors, so it's even with the wrap and can't be seen, as shown.

Separate the cords into four sets, with two short cords and two long cords in each set. Put a clip around each set of cords to keep them together but separate from the other sets. You'll be knotting one set at a time, so leave one set of cords on the board, wind each of the other three sets up, and place them out of the way above the board, as shown.

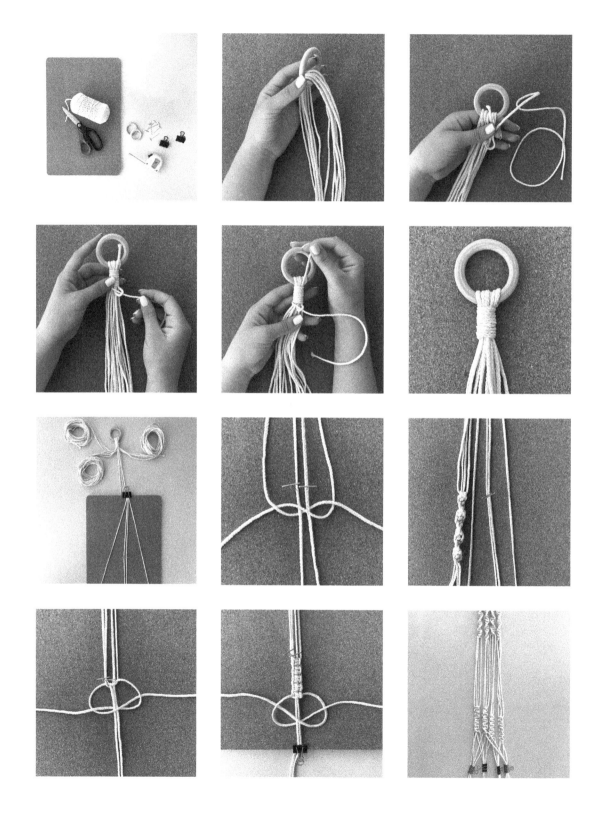

Clip one set of cords to the top of the board to secure it, as shown.

There are two basic knots used to make the macrame hanger shown. The first, the half square knot, creates a corkscrew twist.

As you tie the knots, try to keep the tension even. Tie a half square knot by taking the long cord on the right and crossing it over the top of the two short cords directly below the T-pin and under the long cord to their left, leaving an open bend. Make sure the set of cords you're working with is hanging straight. Separate the four cords in the cord where it crosses over, as shown.

Take the left long cord, crossing it under the two short cords, then over the long cord to their right.

Repeat these two steps until you see three distinct twists in the cord. The twisting pattern will be about four inches long.

Repeat the same pattern on all four sections of cord.

The next knot is a full square knot. Work with one section at a time again. Put the other three sections at the top of the board, out of the way.

Clip one set of cords to the board, just below the twists. Leave eight inches of cord below the half knot. Pin the two short cords to the board. Leave one long cord on either side, the same as before.

The full square knot looks the same, but it doesn't twist. Keep the tension even as you tie. As shown, the left cord bends to the right and goes under the two center short cords just below the T-pin, then over the long cord to the right.

As shown, the right cord goes over the two center cords, then over the long cord to the left.

Repeat these two steps six times. Do the same on the remaining three sets of cords.

One more short set of knots, and the knotting is done!

This short last section of knots helps keep the bottom of the pot stable.

We take two cord sets and clip them to the top of the board just below the knotting. Take two cords from the right side of the cord set on your left, and two cords from the left side of the cords on your right. These are the four closest cords when you place the two sets side by side.

Place the other sets of cord up out of the way.

Leave two inches of straight cord. Pin the two center cords to the board. Leave one cord on either side, the same as before.

Tie the same full square knot, repeating the two steps of the knot four times.

Repeat the same wrap below the wooden ring again, directly below the last four full square knots. Don't leave straight cord below the knots.

Cut the leftover cord so it's even at the length you'd like to see it. There should be enough to leave five or six inches of straight cord.

Gently remove the plastic hangers that came with the plastic garden pot. Tip the pot upside down and let the strands of your trailing succulent fall straight down to keep them untangled. Support the plant gently with your left hand and lift the pot away with your right hand.

Keep the plant upside down while placing the new pot over the roots and soil. Push the new pot over the roots as you tilt the pot on its side, then raise it upright. The strands should stay untangled as you gently spread them over all the sides of the new pot.

If you want to separate a trailing plant, tip it upside down to take it out of its pot. Set the pot aside and hold the plant and its soil with both hands, the strands of the plant hanging down. Gently pull the soil apart to divide the plant. Keep the long strands of the plant hanging down and gently wiggle the soil as you pull the two sides apart. The strands usually untangle easily with only a little manipulation, with a few strands that stay intertwined.

HANGING SUCCULENT KOKEDAMA

For this project, you'll use a ball of hemp cord—I use a forty-eight-pound weight—moss, a spray bottle filled with water, and a four-inch succulent with roots and soil.

Remove the succulent from its plastic garden pot. Dampen the moss so it sticks together easily. Wrap the moss around the soil of the four-inch succulent. The moss will shrink as it dries, so cover the soil generously.

If you're new to this, it's easier to wrap some paddle wire and secure it around the moss ball to make the twine wrap more easily, unless the twine wrap will have a random pattern.

Hemp cord is used to wrap the ball to hold the moss in place.

Put one end of the cord at the bottom of the moss ball and wrap the twine towards you, then directly up, past the succulent, in a straight vertical line to the back. Repeat, keeping the cord always in a straight line from front to back.

I turn the ball slightly to the left with each wrap, keeping my eye on the straight line of the cord. The pattern is the same pattern you see on the outside of a ball of twine. A hole forms naturally on the top for the succulent. You'll see the pattern of the cord forming. Wrap as many times around as you'd like.

Finish off by tying the tails of the first and last wraps securely at the bottom of the Kokedama. Add three pieces of long cord to the sides for hanging. I slip one end of a long cord through intersecting wraps, tie a knot, and bring the double cord up. Repeat with the other two pieces of cord, making six strands coming up for hanging. Raise the ends up, bend them over, and wrap them around and through to create a slip knot.

Water by dipping your Kokedama in water when the moss is completely dry.

CREATING YOUR PLANTER (STEP BY STEP)

DRILLING A DRAINAGE HOLE

You can skip this step if your container has a drainage hole. If it doesn't, and you'd like to add one to make watering easier, here's how to drill one. It's surprisingly easy.

Drilling a drainage hole in a container is really easy. All you need is a power drill with a diamond bit for tile. Tile drill bits have a hollow center and rough outer edges. The size of the drill bit you'll need depends on the size of the pot you've chosen. I drill a ⅜-inch hole for containers up to eight inches. If you're uncertain about the hole size for your container, an easy way to decide is to check the size of the hole in the bottom of a similar-sized terra cotta pot at the garden shop. They always have a drainage hole.

You'll need an electric or battery drill, water, and a diamond drill bit, available at home improvement stores. A half-inch bit is a good size for up to a six-inch pot.

Turn your pot upside down, and hold it securely in place. Pour some water where you'll be drilling the hole.

Set the drill bit at an angle where you want your hole.

Gently press down on the drill. Start drilling slowly at first. Hold the drill steady, because it can slide around a bit when the drill starts. I brace the back of the drill against my body for better control until the bit creates a ridge into the ceramic. Once it's drilling smoothly, reposition the bit flat against the pot and gradually speed up the drill.

Continue adding water around the hole as you drill. Water helps keep the drill bit running smoothly and the ceramic from overheating, and it keeps the dust down. Drill all the way through the bottom of the pot.

If glaze breaks away around the hole on the inside of the pot, it's because the drill bit is getting dull, or the open end of the drill bit may be filled with ceramic bits and dust.

Cover the drainage hole with something to keep the soil from sifting out. Often, I'll take a clump of moss we use around the edges of our planters, or a two- or three-inch piece of window screen. A bit of weed-barrier fabric works well too. Use what you have on hand, but avoid material that deteriorates quickly. Drywall joint tape is a mesh with a sticky back, and it's about the right width to cover a small drainage hole.

Unless you have a way to move a heavy planter effortlessly into place, it's best to set the container where you'd like it to be before you start adding soil and plants.

Some tall containers can be unstable. If a lightweight container has a narrow base, it might wobble or tip when it's bumped or if the wind blows. Make it more stable by putting something heavy in the bottom, such as rocks or bricks.

If a heavy container has a broad, stable base, it's a good idea to add filler to the bottom. Succulent roots are fairly shallow and will not grow to the bottom of a large planter. Extra soil can take a long time to dry out in a large container and will make the plants susceptible to fungus rot. A large pot can be filled up to halfway with a lightweight space filler. Use lightweight, non-biodegradable things you may have on hand that can be repurposed. I use sturdy plastic water bottles with tightly capped lids and large chunks of non-biodegradable packing Styrofoam.

ADDING SOIL

Add enough succulent soil to fill your large container up to about six inches from the top. Set some soil aside to use as you add plants. The soil level will be just below the top of the planter. This high soil level allows air circulation. The soil surface will dry faster to keep the succulents healthy, and moisture won't attract pests like fungus gnats.

Fill the container with soil. If you're adding a dwarf tree or specimen plant, dig a hole in the center of the container and plant it first. A length of rolled newsprint paper wrapped around a larger cactus makes handling and planting it easy. Then continue to follow the next steps. If you're not adding a specimen plant, continue with the planting guide.

If you're adding a large natural element, add it first, the way you would a dwarf tree. Smaller natural elements can be added in place of plants as you go.

I start by planting any trailing succulents along the edge of the container first. This allows the plants to spill over the lip of the container and cascade down as they grow. If they're not planted near the edge, they'll grow over other plants. Add soil under plants as needed to keep the leaves near the top of the container's opening. A wooden dowel can help pack soil around the plants to hold their roots in place.

Next, add low-profile succulents (varieties that won't grow tall). I start planting on the edge of a round container, in a corner for square containers. Keep adding soil as needed under the roots of your plants and just below the edge of the container, being careful to keep all the plant leaves above the soil. Continue planting along the edge of the planter.

The soil can be covered with sand. I use a large silicone drinking straw (available on-line) and a kitchen funnel to direct the sand. Push the staw onto the end of the funnel. Bend the straw and hold it in one hand while you fill the funnel with sand. Pinch and un-pinch the straw to control the sand flow.

Mix equal parts of water and Elmer's School Glue in a plastic container with a pointed tip, and shake well. Squeeze the glue around the sand to keep it in place. It won't damage the plants or affect watering.

CARE TIPS

Water

Add just enough water for the soil to be dry again within three or four days. Drenched soil in deep containers can take days or weeks to dry out, and a damp environment weakens succulents and can attract pests. Less water is best until you can see how long it takes for the soil to dry. A soil water meter can be helpful. The meter should read zero before rewatering. Most large planters only need to be watered once every couple of weeks. Terra cotta is a great choice for succulent planters. It wicks away moisture, stays cool, and helps to keep the soil aerated.

Sun

If you buy succulents from an outdoor garden center in summer without protection overhead, the plants are already used to full sun. Hot midday sun can burn succulents if they've come from greenhouses, where they've been protected from sunburn with shade cloth or with a whitewashed plastic covering. When you bring protected succulents home, their leaves can burn quickly in full sun. Expose greenhouse succulents to full sun gradually. A shallow covered porch can protect them from sunshine directly overhead at midday.

CHAPTER FOUR

OUTDOOR GARDENS

TALL SUCCULENT GARDEN PLANTERS

Planters can add depth and dimension to a space. If you have a small area, adding a tall but narrow planter to define the outer edge of the space can make the area appear larger.

LARGE SUCCULENT GARDEN BOWL PLANTERS

Succulents planted outdoors in pots need a drainage hole because we can't control the amount of water the plant will get. Most outdoor pots already have a drainage hole, but if your pot doesn't, it's easy to drill a hole. Follow the steps in Chapter Three, page 83.

Cover the hole in the bottom of your planter with a piece of screen or weed-barrier cloth. This keeps the soil from filtering out through the hole.

Add enough succulent soil to the planter to bring the bottom leaves of the plants you've chosen up to the rim of the planter when they're planted. Have some extra soil on hand to fill in under plants if needed as you work.

In outdoor planters, a high soil level helps air circulate around the soil's surface, and allows excess water to run off instead of quickly oversaturating the soil when it rains.

Starting with the largest or tallest plant, remove the plant from its plastic garden pot, and set it in the center of the bowl. Extra soil can be mounded a bit under the center plant in a large planter, if you'd like, to help raise it above the other plants you'll be adding.

Press the soil around the center plant to hold it securely upright while you plant the other succulents. Add the remaining plants you've chosen around the bowl. I like to repeat small clusters of the same plant in several large planter areas.

MINI TREE PLANTED WITH SUCCULENTS

Drought-tolerant "Little Ollie" topiary planted with succulents

A beautiful way to show off a drought-tolerant dwarf tree, like *Olea europaea* or "Little Ollie," is to plant it in a tall garden pot surrounded by succulents. Little Ollie is often used as a shrub in drought-tolerant landscapes. It grows slowly and can be pruned like a topiary, with one narrow trunk that branches at the top.

Planting a dwarf tree

Choose a container that's at least twice the size of the garden pot your dwarf tree is in. Most garden pots have drainage holes because moisture can't be controlled outside. If there is no drainage, follow the instructions on page 83 for drilling drainage.

You're ready to plant! Slide the tree out from its garden pot. Add enough soil to the bottom of the new container to raise the tree to an inch below the pot rim. Do not add soil above the tree's roots. Succulents and other drought-tolerant plants do best with plenty of air circulation. Low soil levels keep air from flowing and trap moisture.

After adding soil, add the tree before any other plants. After adding the tree, raise the soil level for the succulents you've chosen. While you add plants, have a bag of succulent soil ready. Take a succulent out of its pot and set it on the soil, near the rim of the pot. Add additional soil under the plant as needed to keep the bottom leaves of the plant level with the rim around the pot.

Continue adding the succulents you've chosen, following the same pattern with the soil. Every area doesn't need to be covered. It also looks nice to add some smooth stones among the succulents.

CARE

Be sure to water your planter whenever the soil is completely dry. Most shrubs and dwarf trees are fine outdoors in full sun, and the little tree will grow and be able to shade the succulents during midday. Until then, protect from full midday sun and frost.

VERTICAL SUCCULENT GARDENS

I love the hand-crafted vertical gardens filled with moss that are available online. They're easy to plant and come in all different shapes and sizes! My favorites are the heart-shaped and the peace sign. A deep picture frame can be repurposed as a vertical garden. A simple shadow box is a great option. The key feature for a vertical garden is a planting depth of two inches or more. It needs to be okay for indoor/outdoor use.

Vertical gardens don't need soil. Succulents grow beautifully in long-strand sphagnum moss without soil. Mist the moss with a spray bottle to make it damp and easy to compact into your vertical garden frame. Press the moss firmly and add more damp

moss. Repeat until the damp moss is even with the top of the shadow box. It's important to press the moss in firmly. As it dries, the moss will shrink a bit.

Secure the moss in place with a fine wire mesh, fishing line, or craft cord. This will hold the moss in place when the garden is hung and watered. Any of these can be attached with an upholstery-style staple gun. Lay the wire mesh, or the cord, in a large grid pattern over the moss-filled vertical garden. Next, staple the ends around the front edge to secure it in place. A thin wooden trim can be added around the edges with small finishing nails.

The moss in the vertical garden will need to be completely dry if planting fresh succulent cuttings, because succulent cuttings are used instead of rooted plants. Fresh succulent cuttings will die if planted in damp soil or moss. The cuttings will grow new roots within a few weeks.

Poke a hole in the dried moss using a sharpened wooden dowel or the sprinkler extractor tool shown.

Leave a stem on each cutting that's just long enough to fit into the moss. Remove a row of leaves if the stem is too short. Save the leaves to grow leaf babies; see page 140 to learn how.

Set the succulent in the little hole in the moss and pin it in place with the U-shaped fern pin. The pin can secure the stem or a leaf without damaging the plant. Continue to add succulent cuttings side by side. If it's difficult to pin the succulent, use the floral adhesive. The floral adhesive is used on the bottom of the leaves, not the fresh-cut stems of the succulents. I use a little trick with the adhesive—have it touch the sides of other plants, the inside edge of the vertical garden, or some of the cord. This really helps to secure the plants.

CARE

Wait two weeks to water your freshly planted vertical garden. Hang it where the plants get hours of direct morning or late afternoon sunshine to keep their colors vibrant and the plants compact. Water by drenching the vertical garden with cool water. The watering schedule will depend on your climate. Be sure not to water until the moss is completely dry or the plant leaves have a slightly leathery feel.

SUCCULENT PALLET GARDEN

You'll need a wooden pallet, succulent soil mix, long-strand sphagnum moss, a Saw-zall-style reciprocating saw or a sharp hand saw and lots of energy, a drill, wood screws, a hammer and nails, weed-barrier fabric, and an upholstery stapler with staples.

Remove every other board from one side of the pallet. Use the removed boards to create the bottom of each planting box. Pre-drill holes for each screw, and affix the removed boards underneath the remaining ones to form planting boxes.

Trim weed-barrier cloth to line the inside of each planting box and secure with staples.

Add soil to each planter box until it's just below the top edges. The succulents need to be planted with root-touching closeness to stay compact. It's a good idea to keep an eye on how plant colors and textures flow from one shelf to another. You'll want splashes of color here and there throughout the pallet. Use a variety of shapes, sizes, and textures. Be sure to incorporate some hanging plants. Use taller succulents for the top shelf. Many design elements for landscaping from the beginning of the book apply to larger planters like this pallet garden.

SUCCULENT ORB

Moss orbs for planting can be found online and in garden centers. Just be sure you're buying garden quality, or it may be filled with newspaper instead of moss. If you'd like to make it yourself, it's easy.

Succulents grow beautifully in long-strand sphagnum moss, so you won't need succulent potting mix to make an orb, just moss and a spray bottle filled with water to keep the moss damp. I use craft or fishing line, but a thin cord works to form the ball. A six-inch orb turns into eight inches with succulents. You'll need a chain and a ring or an S-hook for hanging.

Dampen the moss and form it into a firm ball to make the moss orb. Wrap fishing line or thin cord around the ball to hold its shape. Tuck and tie the wrap, so it's secure. Add another layer of moss, keeping it damp to ensure the orb is dense and firm when it dries. Wrap with the cord or nylon line, moss again, then tie the wrap to secure it. Continue this until the moss ball is the size you'd like. Wait for the moss to dry to add a chain and hook and to plant it.

After the ball has dried, push a half-inch sharpened wooden dowel through the center of the ball. Pull the dowel out and feed the end of a chain through the hole. Push it through with the dowel. Add an S-hook or ring to one end of the chain. Secure the end of 24-gauge paddle wire through a link in the chain at the bottom of the orb. Pull it up and through the chain at the top of the ball, then back down on the opposite side and through the bottom of the chain again. Repeat on the opposite side of the orb to secure the chain and moss ball with four wires that divide the surface into quarters. Secure the wire with a few twists at the bottom and tuck the ends into the moss.

Planting a succulent orb for the first time can be tricky, but I'm here to show you how! Plant the bottom half first. Choose your succulent cuttings from succulents with a rosette shape. If you choose plants with stems that grow long and don't do well being cut back, your ball will lose its round shape. I choose echeveria, sempervivum, sedum, graptopetalum, and pachyphytum. Crassula grow long quickly and need to be cut back, and their stems can get woody, but they are pretty. If you choose to add trailing succulents, think about placing them as you're finishing up the orb. This will keep them from becoming tangled as you plant around them.

Set the moss orb on a table upside down. Put a 20-gauge wire through the stem and thread it halfway onto the wire. Bend the wire down along the sides of the stem. Make a small dip on the bottom of the orb in the center. Put the succulent stem in the dip. Push the wire through the ball and into the side of the orb in the direction of one of the four wires that secure the chain. Twist the ends around that wire, cut the excess, and tuck in the ends.

Add more succulent cuttings, repeating this process. It's good to have some succulents on the bottom wired in to keep the plants secure until they root. Others can be pinned in place with fern pins. The wired succulents will help to keep the others in place until they all have roots.

Once the bottom half of the orb is planted, hang it from the top and plant the top half the same way as the bottom. If you have little spaces, it's fun to add smaller succulents. They can be added with floral adhesive applied to the bottoms of their leaves (not the stems) and clump four to five strands of trailing succulents. Secure trailing succulents with a fern pin. They lie flat and cascade over other plants, and eventually below the orb.

CARE

Morning sun or late afternoon sun is best for succulents. Shelter from direct noon sun to avoid sunburn. You may need to rotate the orb every few weeks for equal sunlight. Drench the orb by dipping in cool water, only once every few weeks. The moss stays wet for an extended time. Hang to drip dry. Use a soil moisture meter to know when to water. It will read zero when it's time to water.

SUCCULENT PLANTED CHAIR

Choose a chair with a rush seat if you can find one. They're great for drainage! In any event, be sure to use a chair with a removable seat. A padded seat is fine as long as it can be removed. Take off the rush seat and reattach it underneath. If you use a padded seat, toss it and attach some chicken wire underneath the seating area with an upholstery stapler.

Continue adding plants in clusters. Start from the edges and work toward the center. Plants should be planted with root-touching closeness to limit their growth. Add pops of color, cluster smaller plants, and add a few succulents that will trail or grow over the edge and plants with varying shapes and textures.

SUCCULENT RAIN GUTTER PLANTER

If you've chosen a metal rain gutter, you'll need to seal it with a protective clear coat. Copper, for example, can weaken the new roots of some plants. Be sure to check the directions to allow the sealer to cure completely. I waited three days before planting after sealing the rain gutter.

Drill large holes every couple of feet for drainage, and place a patch of weed-barrier fabric above each one.

Fill with succulent soil all the way to the top of the gutter. Keep in mind that it will compact as plants are added. This also prevents any potential pooling of rainwater, which can damage the plants.

Add groupings of plants. Remember that succulents grow naturally in clusters. Artistically incorporate some more prominent plants as well as some hanging plants. Use design elements of color, texture, and size.

Use sphagnum moss along the front edge of the rain gutter. This will help keep the soil in place and looks nice.

SUCCULENT RAIN CHAIN GARDENS

With the growing popularity of rain chains, they're available at large garden centers and online in all kinds of pretty styles. Compare prices. The prices vary considerably for the same item from one shop to another. Choose a rain chain that is wide enough to handle an assortment of succulents.

You'll also need succulent soil and moss.

Begin by putting an egg-sized piece of long-strand sphagnum moss at the bottom of each pot. This will keep the soil from washing out during watering.

No extra soil needs to be added to the rain chain. Take the succulents from their plastic garden pots and arrange them in the rain chain with root-touching closeness so they'll stay put. I didn't add any moss around the edges.

Start planting at the top of the rain chain. It keeps soil from falling on the plants below. And the weight of the rain chain will steady the containers if plants aren't evenly balanced.

Hang the chain in a spot that gets plenty of morning or late afternoon sun. Avoid direct midday summer sun.

SECTION II

SUCCULENT KNOW-HOW

CHAPTER FIVE

SUCCULENT CARE

HOW OFTEN DO SUCCULENTS NEED WATER?

Succulents are quite independent. They're perfectly at home with minimal water. Their roots soak up moisture quickly and store it in their stems and leaves to survive until the next rain. Rain evaporates quickly in arid climates because of wind. They grow naturally in arid climates, where many plants can't survive. Wind is constantly eroding the rocky landscape, making the soil coarse. Coarse soil is fast-draining. Because there is less plant life, the soil also has less organic material and nutrients.

Succulents grow well in this fast-draining soil. As much as succulents need water, they also need a drying-out period. Allowing succulent soil to dry out completely and stay dry for a bit mimics their natural environment. Their roots actually need a break from wet soil. It gives them a chance to breathe and helps keep the plant healthy.

Before I had succulents, my house was filled with tropicals, and they thrive on water and nutrients. It's a completely different mindset when you're taking care of succulents. It's natural to want to nurture a beautiful plant, to water and fertilize it and fuss over it. But succulents seem to thrive on a little neglect.

How often to water succulents depends on how fast their soil dries. The kind of soil you have is one factor, and weather is another. If it's hot, dry, or windy, water evaporates quickly. But if it's cold, humid, or there's little air circulation, it can take days. Knowing how often to water takes a little experimenting with your soil and checking your local weather. That's why there's no right answer for, "How often should I water my succulents?"

It's easier to kill succulents by overwatering than underwatering, so if you're unsure, lean toward underwatering. Succulents naturally survive dry spells.

WATERING ACCESSORIES

WATERING CAN

If you love plants, you'll probably have fun browsing garden shops or online for cute indoor watering cans. I look for a long neck with a narrow spout. This style helps to get most of the water on the soil, less on succulent leaves and the floor.

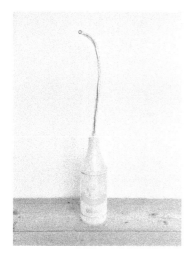

WATERING BOTTLES FOR HANGING PLANTS

A plastic squeeze bottle with a long, curved, position-able tube makes watering hanging plants and plants on high shelves easy. I found mine online, made by UBloom.

PORTABLE PUMP GARDEN SPRAYER

A portable pump garden sprayer may be just the thing for you to avoid dragging a hose around or carrying a watering can. I like the gallon-sized ITISLL with a brass wand and adjustable nozzle. It can also be used to spray pests with neem oil, Dawn dish soap, or other garden concoctions.

HOSE NOZZLE

If you're watering lots of succulents outdoors, here's what the pros use to make watering easy. It's called the

Red Dramm 1000 Water Breaker Nozzle. It's practically a secret, and the name sounds like it was made for Harry Potter. It's bright red plastic, and you can find it online or at better garden centers. I love it because it has one thousand tiny holes that create a dense but gentle shower that's beautiful to watch. It also won't damage tender plants or dislodge soil. If you have a long hose, adding a screw-on valve to your Dramm nozzle will help turn the water on and off when you're away from the hose bib. Dramm also makes an attachment for watering out-of-reach outdoor hanging plants.

SOIL MOISTURE METER

A finger makes a pretty good soil moisture meter. Push your finger a couple of inches into the soil to feel if it's dry. If the soil feels cool, it's still damp. If you're unsure or want a second opinion, a good quality soil moisture meter can help. A soil moisture meter reads zero when the soil is dry. And that's how dry succulent soil should be before rewatering. Moisture meters are available online and at most garden centers. Beware, though, the ones that are cheaply made aren't reliable. Don't be tempted to check to see if the meter works or how wet it thinks water is by putting it in water. It won't read correctly, and doing this could ruin it. They're designed to detect moisture in soil only.

HOW TO WATER SUCCULENTS

I'm often asked how to water succulents and how much water to give them.

After years in succulent greenhouses, I've seen a rhythm to watering succulents out-doors. It may help uncertain beginners until you find what works best for you in your climate. When watering outdoors, attach the Red Dramm garden nozzle to the hose (with the on/off valve beneath it). Turn the hose on full force and flash-water your plants by passing the Red Dramm garden nozzle over every succulent pot briefly. This helps to prep the soil to easily soak up more water.

Go back a second time around, and water everything for two seconds (that's about how long it takes to count quickly to eight). This is usually enough time to wet the soil top to bottom. Then turn the water off, take a deep breath and look around. The gar-den smells amazing when it's just been watered! And the succulents look so beautiful and happy.

It takes some experimenting to learn how quickly your soil absorbs water. Once you've finished watering, it's a good idea to check a few plants to see how wet their soil is. Press your finger deep into the soil. If it's wet two inches down, you're good to go.

If your plants are in plastic garden pots, another way to check the soil is to tip a pot and gently slide the plant out along with all its soil, just to make sure the water seeped through.

It might surprise you to see that only the top half-inch or so of soil is wet. That's because some soils repel water when they're completely dry. Water can flow down the inside edge of the pot and out through the bottom. So, water flowing from the pot's drainage holes doesn't always mean the soil's wet. With a bit of experience, you'll learn how much water it takes to saturate your soil.

When you're new to growing succulents, check the soil daily after a watering to find the "dry-out period," or how long it takes the soil to dry out. Succulents need completely dry soil for one to three days before being rewatered. The hotter the weather, the less time they can go without water.

After several watering periods, you'll know how often to water. Soil shouldn't stay wet for more than three to four days. If the soil is still saturated after three days, cut your watering time back. This is important because, if the soil stays soaked for more than three or four days, your succulents could get fungus and begin to rot.

When temperatures are high, and soil dries faster, soil may dry in one or two days. See if watering more deeply keeps the soil wet longer. Water only after the soil is completely dry.

If your succulents begin to wither because you forgot to water them, saturate the soil, then wait for it to dry before you water again. Succulent roots can start to atrophy or wither if left without water during prolonged hot spells. When you water, water as you usually would. Don't overwater to compensate. Weakened plants are more susceptible to pests and fungus damage from overwatering.

Because succulents store water inside their stems and leaves, another way to know if they need water is by the feel and look of their leaves. Hydrated succulent leaves look plump and feel firm. The leaves will spring back if you cup your hand around the plant gently, pressing the leaves together, then letting them go. If the plant doesn't feel stiff and the leaves don't spring back quickly, the plant needs water. If leaves have prune-like wrinkles or they feel leathery when you cup your hand around the plant, it's time to water. Succulents handle high temperatures better when their leaves are plump with water.

It's always best to water first thing in the morning. If the weather's hot, the sun heats up the soil. Watering hot soil damages roots and can kill succulents. And watering in the morning gives water a chance to evaporate off the leaves before the sun goes down. Water that collects on leaves and sits all night can cause black fungus to grow on the leaves. This might not be a concern if you live in a hot, dry climate and water evaporates without sunshine.

Another tip for growing succulents in scorching climates is to plant your succulents in terra cotta garden pots, instead of plastic or hard-fired ceramic pots. Plastic pots and glazed ceramic containers hold heat like an oven that exacerbates high temperatures.

I don't mist succulents. I think watering succulents by misting is a bit like dumping water on your head to quench your thirst. Mist is so fine that it doesn't pour down onto the soil and get enough water to the roots where it's absorbed. A fine mist of water that just sits on succulent leaves without evaporating during the day can cause fungus or root rot. I've found that a quick pass with the Dramm nozzle (I call it flash watering) is better than misting for succulents with tender new roots that aren't mature enough for totally saturated soil. Some rare cacti and succulents need only a few drops of water. For these unusual plants, it's best to apply water on the soil, directly above the root ball, with a dropper.

Graptoveria 'Jules'

Succulent roots absorb water quickly and store it in their stems and leaves. When the leaves are filled with water and the soil is still wet, the plant draws more water and overfills the leaves. This makes the leaves fall off easily. Also, the leaf edges of overwatered succulents often become yellow-tinged and get a translucent look about them. These are signs that your plant is drowning.

Many succulents have beautiful yellow leaves. Don't assume that every yellow succulent is overwatered. Some succulents are variegated, with leaves that have yellow and other colors. One succulent I'm thinking of is the Graptoveria 'Jules'. It has an outer row of yellow leaves, and its other leaves are pink!

We can't talk about watering succulents without mentioning soil and air circulation. Choosing a fast-draining cactus and succulent soil, and having good air circulation, will solve most overwatering problems. A gentle breeze or fan helps wet soil evaporate more quickly. If you've accidentally overwatered, a fan can help avoid fungus rot. Air circulation keeps fungus away and succulents happy. See the section on soil to learn more about selecting succulent soil for your climate.

I'm sometimes asked if succulents should be "bottom-watered" by setting plants on a tray filled with water. Succulents specifically grown for garden shows are often bottom-watered to avoid water spots on their leaves. But plants that sit in a tray of water can absorb too many salts or other minerals that may become toxic over time. It takes a water expert to know all the chemicals in local water. I haven't seen long-term, large-scale bottom-watering work successfully in succulent greenhouses in Southern California. Every location is different, so it may work for you.

If rain is in the forecast and your outdoor succulents are dry, skip watering. Unless your weather is scorching hot and dry, succulents can survive a week or more with dry soil. Succulents love rainwater!

I've seen thousands of succulent plants thrown out by professional growers because of unexpected rain that came shortly after the plants had been watered. Rain or humidity can keep the soil saturated for more than three to four days. That's sometimes all it takes for succulents to get fungus rot.

Soil dries more slowly when temperatures are cooler. Experiment with shorter watering times as temperatures drop, until you get the right amount of water for the soil to dry within three to four days.

If you have cold-hardy succulents and freezing temperatures are forecast, don't water outdoor succulents. Succulents have a better chance of surviving temperatures below 32 degrees Fahrenheit if their soil is dry and they have less water in their leaves, stems, and roots.

Cold-hardy succulents go dormant in winter and don't need water. Don't be tempted to water them when the weather is dry but freezing. They'll get water later, from melting snow, as the weather warms. Cold-hardy succulents must be protected from slushy snow during warm spells—it can saturate the ground and later refreeze. Turn to the sections on soil and planting for tips on well-draining soil.

A quick note about pots with saucers. Some great-looking pots come with cute saucers to collect water. Be sure to tip standing water out of the saucer after watering. If the saucer is filled with water, it keeps the soil damp. A great fix is to put decorative rocks or pebbles in the saucer, then set the pot on top!

What if you've found the perfect pot, and it doesn't have drainage holes? It's okay. If you know how to care for succulents, remember that the soil will take longer to dry. Compensate by giving less water. Water just enough for the roots to soak it up within three days. Or, as mentioned in the section on Preparing Containers, it's easy to drill a drainage hole, so refer to that simple step-by-step DIY guide if needed.

THE IMPORTANCE OF SUNLIGHT

Succulents get their beautiful colors from the same chemicals that give fruits and vegetables their rainbow of colors. Succulents come in all the colors we see in produce—blueberries, red cherries, purple eggplant, and yellow and orange bell peppers, to name only a few. Once fruits and vegetables are ripe, they don't need sunlight to keep from turning back to green. On the other hand, succulents need lots of sunlight to keep their bright, vibrant color.

Sometimes people think their succulents are doing great because they've grown so tall and they're stretching out in all directions, but they're mistaken. Succulents without enough sunshine are stressed. They grow tall in search of sunlight. Stressed succulents lose their flower-like shape and become elongated. It's called *etiolation*. When succulents have enough sunlight, they're compact, and their leaves grow in a close pattern, stacked one above another. The stem is barely visible between their leaves.

I've noticed that often the first sign that a succulent needs more light is that its leaves lie very flat instead of holding their naturally cupped shape. Next, the color in the leaves fades and begins to turn green. New leaves growing in the center at the top of the plant stay small as they use all their energy to grow skyward in search of more sunlight. The leaves look sparse along the long, etiolated stem.

If the succulent doesn't get more sunshine, it's more susceptible to pests. The plant will look more like a weed than a succulent as its leaves become smaller and sparser. And the plant will eventually die.

More sunshine can save the plant, but won't return it to its compact shape. Once the plant regains color and the leaves are full-sized again, cut the stem down so the plant is about three inches tall. The new growth will be healthy. Save the leaves from the cut stem and refer to the section on succulent propagation to learn how to use them to propagate new plants.

The amount of direct sunshine your succulents need depends on the intensity of the heat and sun where you live. If the sun is too intense, succulent leaves sunburn. Sunburnt leaves have large, uneven brown spots that appear, usually a day after too much strong sun. These spots won't heal, but as new leaves grow, your plants will be beautiful again.

If you live in a desert climate where the sun is scorching, your succulents need protection from intense midday sun. But shade is not enough to keep them beautiful. Place the plants where the sun will shine directly on them early in the morning, and they'll have indirect sunlight the rest of the day. A covered patio, sunshade, or patio umbrella can protect succulents as the sun climbs higher in the sky and becomes more intense. All shade options also need good air circulation to keep succulents healthy.

Most garden centers have mesh screens overhead that protect plants from the harsh noon sun. Often nursery center succulents are placed indoors, without natural sunlight, for short-term shopping convenience. Don't mistake this for acceptable growing conditions. It's not. Succulents displayed this way aren't intended to stay on the shelf for any length of time.

The south side of any yard gets the most hours of sunlight during the day. If you live where the sun is harsh, it's important to place plants where they can be sheltered from the midday sun and increase exposure gradually.

Outdoor nurseries often mark the south-facing side of plants in the nursery yard. This is so you can place the plant facing the same direction when you get it home to avoid sunburn on the side that's not used to southern exposure.

Succulents that have been in a greenhouse, protected from full sun, or kept indoors in temporary shade, can sunburn easily when they're exposed to full sun. But most succulents build up an ability to take more direct sunlight without sunburn if they're exposed to it gradually. Succulents growing outside in the spring when the sun is mild get more sun exposure as the season changes to summer. Sheltered succulents brought home during midsummer can only handle full early morning sun. They should be moved out of direct sunshine before midday. Gradually increase their sun exposure each day for about a week before you set them outside all day.

A simple way to remember not to expose greenhouse succulents to harsh summer sun is by comparing their sun exposure to yours. It doesn't take long to get a sunburn the first time in the summer sun without sun protection. But if you're gradually spending a little more time in the sun, you can usually avoid sunburn. I've found that greenhouse succulents have similar sun sensitivity. However, most succulents will need ongoing strong midday and afternoon sun protection in harsh, desert-like climates.

Succulents ordered online have been in a dark box for two to seven days on arrival and will likely be stressed from lack of sunshine. They can easily regain their color with gradual exposure to more sunlight. Direct morning sun is mild. Gradually introduce them to more direct sunlight to prevent sunburn. It can take two weeks for succulents that have lost color to regain full color.

Many succulents grow naturally in harsh, cold climates and in full sun. The key is selecting climate-appropriate succulents and placing them outside in springtime, or gradually exposing them to more sunlight during the summer months.

If you're making a greenhouse for your succulents, you'll need a roof that filters sunlight but keeps out rain, and openings to allow lots of air circulation. Commercial greenhouses for hot climates often have mesh sides that filter harsh sunlight, but allow air circulation. They're usually made with PVC pipe framing and covered with whitewashed plastic. Mesh siding is added a few feet from the bottoms of the plastic walls around the greenhouse. The plants are kept on tables, not shelves, to ensure that all the plants have the same amount of sunlight.

I've discovered that grow lights work well as a supplement, but aren't enough to replace natural sunlight indoors in winter. Some succulent collectors say they success-fully grow succulents indoors with only fluorescent lighting, like the T5 grow lights. I haven't found grow lights that are able to give enough light for succulents to retain their compact shape and intense colors that come from natural sunlight. If you're using grow lights in place of sunshine, eight to twelve hours a day is recommended. Succulents need about five hours of rest from light. You may have success experimenting with longer hours or various lightbulbs.

SUCCULENTS THAT DO WELL WITH LESS SUNLIGHT

If you have succulents outdoors in shade, or indoors without a lot of sunlight streaming on them through the window, these are the succulents I'd recommend:

Name	Height
Aeonium haworthii—Kiwi aeonium	2–3 feet
Agave attenuata—Fox tail agave	3–4 feet
Aloe—Aloe 'Doran Black' (sometimes called Dorian Black)	6–8 inches
Aloe maculata—Soap aloe	1–2 feet
Aloe barbadensis—Aloe vera	1–2 feet
Aloe arborescens—Krantz aloe	10 feet
Beaucarnea recurrata—Ponytail palm	10 feet
Ceropegia woodii—String of hearts	vine
Crassula multicava—Fairy crassula	under 6 inches
Crassula ovata—Jade plant	3–6 feet

Gasteria 'Little Warty'	under 6 inches
Haworthia fasciata—Zebra plant	8 inches
Haworthia cooperi—Window plant	under 6 inches
Haworthia cuspidata f. variegata—Window plant, variegated	under 6 inches
Haworthiopsis viscosa or *Haworthia viscosa*	under 6 inches
Hoya—Wax plants	vine
Peperomia	under 6 inches
Rhipsalidopsis gaertneri or *Hatiora gaertneri*—Easter cactus	vine
Sansevieria—Snake plant	3 feet
Schlumbergera bridgesii—Christmas cactus	vine
Sedum (now *Hylotelephium*) *sieboldii*—October Daphne	6–8 inches
Sedum ternatum—Woodland sedum	under 6 inches
Sedum morganianum—Donkey tail	vine
Sedum sieboldii—October Daphne stonecrop	9 inches
Senecio radicans—String of bananas	vine
Senecio rowleyanus—String of pearls	vine
Tillandsia—Air plants	sizes vary
Zamioculcas zamiifolia—ZZ plant or aroid palm	2–3 feet

SUCCULENTS THAT SURVIVE FREEZING TEMPERATURES

Many succulents die if the water in their leaves, stems, or roots freezes. Winter or cold-hardy succulents survive freezing cold temperatures. They do best planted in the ground or in large pots. Plant early in the spring when there's no risk of freezing. This gives their roots time to mature and become well established in the soil before winter.

Succulents do best if they're in the right-size container. The container should have a space of about one inch between the roots and the container. Deep soil can help insulate their roots from the cold.

It's always essential to have well-draining soil for succulents, and cold-hardy succulents are no exception. They can take freezing temperatures, but they will rot if they sit in wet soil. This can be tricky because snow melts and turns to water and slush, then often refreezes in the ground.

There's a simple test to determine if your soil is quick-draining. Dig a hole that's a foot deep and a foot wide; be sure you've removed any loose soil. Fill the hole to the top with water and keep track of how long it takes for the water to drain. If all the water drains within ten minutes, you have fast-draining soil.

One way to overcome soggy soil caused by melting snow is to ensure that your succulents are planted on a slope or mound of well-draining soil.

Another idea is to dig a one-foot-deep meandering trench to create a dry riverbed and fill it with various-sized rocks. Plant the succulents along the top edges. Create a rock garden and plant succulents near the rocks.

Along with the rocks, add coarse gravel to well-draining soil.

If your cold-hardy succulents are planted in pots, make sure to choose large pots to help insulate the roots from the cold.

Several types of succulents can endure the harsh cold. They come from areas with below-freezing temperatures and scorching summers. They must be planted in spring before the heat of summer, or in late summer to early fall, for their roots to be well established before extreme temperatures.

Name	Height
Agave havardiana—Harvard's agave	2 feet
Agave parryi—Parry's or artichoke agave	3 feet
Agave palmeri—Palmers century plant	3 feet
Aloe humilis—Spider aloe	12 inches
Aloe blue elf	18 inches
Cotyledon undulata—Silver ruffles	19 inches
Delosperma—Ice plant	under 6 inches
Echeveria lilacina	under 6 inches
Echeveria runyonii—'Topsy Turvy'	under 6 inches
Euphorbia royleanna—Royle's spurge	5 feet
Graptopetalum bellus	under 6 inches
Orostachys—Chinese dunce cap	under 6 inches
Sedum spurium—Dragon's blood stonecrop	under 6 inches
Sedum sieboldii—October Daphne stonecrop	9 inches
Sedum spathulifolium—Broadleaf stonecrop	8 inches

Sedum makinoi "Ogon"—Golden Japanese stonecrop	under 6 inches
Sedum tetractinum—Chinese stonecrop "Coral Reef"	under 6 inches
Sempervivum & Jovibarba—Hens and chicks	under 6 inches
Titanopsis calcarea	under 6 inches
Yucca baccata—Banana or datil	3–4 feet
Yucca elata—Soaptree yucca	15 feet
Yucca filimentosa—Adam's needle	10 feet
Yucca glauca—Soapweed yucca	20 inches
Yucca harrimaniae—Spanish bayonet	12 inches
Yucca rostrata—Blue Yucca	5–15 feet

SUCCULENT SOIL

Everyone you ask will have a different opinion on which soil is best for succulents. This is true partly because succulent needs vary depending on the climate and the variety of succulents. Even a few miles can make a difference in heat and humidity. And it's partly because growing plants is a science which involves experimenting and learning.

It isn't necessary to create your own succulent soil anymore, because many high-quality succulent and cactus soils are available today. Off-the-shelf succulent and cactus soils from garden centers are excellent choices. They're mixed to be lightweight and well-draining. And they're often customized for the region where they're sold.

Volcanic Rock (scoria)

Pumice

Horticultural Sand

Coconut Coir Chunks

Coconut Coir

Peat Moss

Crushed Granite/Poultry Grit

Quick Dry Stall Dryer

Perlite

I live in Southern California, minutes away from many large and small succulent growers. Most of them use huge bags of commercial cactus and succulent soil mix as their base. They add perlite or pumice to help the soil drain and dry faster in our humid climate. Nurseries use this richer soil to grow baby to gallon-size succulents.

You may find that your plants do best with an ingredient or two added to your packaged soil mix. It's easy to adjust packaged succulent and cactus soils for your climate when you know how the amendments affect the soil.

I'll explain what the various ingredients in succulent soil do, so you can adjust your soil mix to grow beautiful succulents in your climate.

Inorganic material is added to improve drainage. Organic material aids growth.

INORGANIC

Perlite

Perlite is made from obsidian, a natural volcanic glass. It's crushed and heated to nearly 1700 degrees. Any moisture in it expands, making it pop and turning it white and porous. Perlite is used to lighten soil and help it drain faster. If you live in a hot, dry climate, add less. It comes in three textures: coarse, medium, and fine. The coarser sizes create the fastest drainage. Perlite improves aeration by creating spaces in the soil. It's so lightweight that it tends to float to the top of soil eventually and can easily wash away. It doesn't decompose, and it has no nutrient value.

Pumice

Pumice is a natural volcanic mineral. It's the stone often used in spas to soften feet. Pumice is used to lighten soil and help it drain faster. It creates spaces in the soil to improve aeration. Pumice is heavier than perlite, so it stays mixed into the soil instead of floating to the top, and helps to anchor top-heavy succulents. It doesn't decompose, has no nutrient value, and adds minerals to the soil. Pumice is available in big bags under the Dry Stall or Quick Dry brand names at animal feed stores. Don't confuse this with Stall Dry; they're entirely different. Stall Dry is clay-based and will ruin your soil. Pumice can be purchased in garden centers and online. My favorite brand for selecting the size of the pumice stones is General Pumice Products.

Horticulture Sand

This has a much larger grit than regular sand. It won't stick together like fine sand. Horticulture or Coarse sand creates space that increases the oxygen to the roots. Don't confuse this with playground sand, which is fine and dense. Horticulture sand is heavy, and some growers say it doesn't increase drainage. You'll need to decide for yourself. It won't drift to the top of the soil like perlite. Several of our growers say that adding horticulture sand to soil mix intensifies the color of the succulents. It doesn't decompose, and it has no nutrient value.

Crushed Granite or Poultry Grit

Crushed granite and poultry grit are irregularly shaped. This keeps them from sticking together. It creates spaces in the soil to increase oxygen around the plant's roots. Poultry grit is made of tiny rocks, shells, and crushed granite; it's generally smaller than coarse horticulture sand.

Volcanic Rock (Scoria)

Scoria is a dark-colored volcanic rock ranging from black to shades of grey, brown, or dark red. Scoria is heavier than pumice. Some say plants grow slower in scoria. It's porous and fast-draining. No nutrient value. It will not decompose.

Rocks & Pebbles

Most succulent growers agree that adding rocks or pebbles to the bottom of containers does not improve drainage. If water sits between the rocks, bacteria grows, and dampness attracts pests.

ORGANIC

Coconut

Coir comes from coconuts. It resembles peat moss, but soaks up water faster and retains more moisture than peat. If you live in a drier climate, this may be an advantage. Coir has no nutrient value, so fertilizing is essential. We've found that succulent plants don't grow as quickly with coir. Coir decomposes over time.

Coconut coir chunks are larger chunks than the coir from coconuts. It holds more moisture, so it's not fast-draining enough for succulents. Still, it's great for growing hoya plants, often grown with succulents.

Coconut coir is considered sustainable because it comes from coconut shells. But it may not be entirely eco-friendly because the manufacturing process uses lots of water and creates pollutants.

Peat Moss

Lightweight peat improves oxygen in the soil for roots. It holds water and dries quickly. Peat tends to repel water when it's dry. Often succulent nurseries and many potting soils use peat as a soil base and add other ingredients. It has some nutrients, but fertilizing is recommended. It decomposes over time. There's some environmental concern about over-harvesting peat bogs and the sustainability of peat.

WHEN TO PLANT AND REPOT

Plant succulents in the garden and repot overgrown succulents during the season when they're actively growing. This gives their roots a chance to become well established before the weather changes and they become more stressed.

Popular Succulent Soil Mixes

These are a few popular well-draining succulent soil combinations. The mixes with more organic material drain a bit slower.

- 50 percent inorganic coarse material and 50 percent organic
- 10 percent inorganic coarse material, 50 percent perlite, 40 percent potting soil
- 35 percent inorganic coarse material, 35 percent perlite, 30 percent potting soil

Dick Wright's Echeveria Soil Mix:

- 10 scoops Canadian peat, 10 scoops perlite, 1 part vermiculite flakes, 2 scoops sand (washed builder's supply sand ¼-inch and less)

Aloe Soil Mix:

- 6 scoops pumice, 2 scoops peat moss, 2 scoops washed builder's sand, ¼-inch and less

An easy way to test soil drainage is to wet the soil, then squeeze it into a ball. If it falls apart, it should have good drainage. If it holds its shape, it's slow-draining.

Another common test to see if garden soil has good drainage is to dig a hole one square foot deep and wide and remove any loose soil. Fill the hole to the top with water and track how long it takes to drain. If all the water drains within ten minutes, the soil is fast-draining soil.

SUCCULENT PESTS

Not every garden pest likes succulents, but a few do. It's a smart idea to check your plants for pests before you buy them. Keep new plants away from the others until you've carefully checked the stems and tops and bottoms of their leaves for pests.

Most succulent pests look like tiny specks or spots on the leaves. Finding pests early makes getting rid of them easy. Recheck your plants when you're watering them, so you can catch little problems before they become overwhelming.

Healthy plants don't have as many pest problems. Allow the soil to dry out before watering. It helps to keep succulents healthy. Too much fertilizer can also attract pests.

MEALYBUG

Mealy looks like tiny bits of sticky white cotton. It's usually found where the leaves attach to the plant's stem. Mealy are good at hiding in tiny crevices. It can also be in the soil. Take the plant out of its pot to see if the bugs have spread to the roots. Mealybugs often look like random dime-sized patches of white dust on the sides of soil. Mealy can spread from one plant to another, so it's best to isolate a plant that's being treated.

FUNGUS

One type of fungus, called black mold, lives on the sticky residue from succulent pests. Once you kill the other pests, the black mold, sometimes called sooty mold, clears up.

Other types of fungus are attracted to water. It's good to know how to stop fungus because succulents are particularly sensitive to fungus rot. Fungus grows from microscopic spores that float easily on air, and when they land in a damp place, like wet soil or water trapped between succulent leaves, they grow. Good air circulation can help to compensate for overwatering. It speeds up evaporation and can prevent fungus rot. Once fungus rot damages a plant, it's often too late to save it. Fungus is preventable by treating plants with a solution of neem oil. Sprinkle cinnamon on top of the soil.

FUNGUS GNATS

Fungus gnats are tiny flying pests that are a sign of overwatering. Fungus gnats will appear out of nowhere if you overwater a plant, then it sits in wet soil for more than a few days without good air circulation. They hover around damp soil, where they lay their eggs. Allowing the soil to dry completely and remain dry for three days before rewatering can kill off a gnat infestation. If you live in an arid climate and your plants can't go days with dry soil, you probably will never have a problem with fungus or fungus gnats. Diatomaceous earth, neem oil, or Dawn dish soap will all kill fungus gnats. Some of my best growers sprinkle ground cinnamon on top of the soil.

APHIDS

Aphids are another tiny flying pest. They come in various colors and are usually found in clusters on the leaves and stems. They have a waxy coating that keeps moisture in their bodies, so contact with diatomaceous earth damages their waxy coat, and they die of dehydration. Spraying them with soapy water until the plant is dripping wet will dehydrate and kill them on contact. Neem oil also kills aphids.

SCALE

Scale looks like small brown dots or bumps on leaves and stems. They have a waxy coating that keeps moisture in their bodies. Damaging this coating kills scale. Scale can move from plant to plant in its crawler stage, so if you find scale on one succulent, check nearby plants too. Neem oil, mild Dawn dish soap (it's not ammonia-based), or isopropyl alcohol on a cotton swab can remove scale from the leaves.

Saturate the leaves, top and bottom, and the stem with a neem oil solution or a mild dish soap like Dawn mixed with water—let it drip down into the soil. Dead scale bugs will stick to the plant. Isopropyl alcohol also kills scale, and saturating a cotton pad with alcohol and cleaning the leaves helps remove the bugs.

SPIDER MITES

Spider mites look like colonies of tiny, crawling, red-colored specks. They make webs. Spider mites, like many pests, have a waxy coating that keeps moisture in their bodies. Using mild dish soap and water or a neem oil solution damages the waxy coating on spider mites, and that's how it kills them.

THRIPS

Thrips (even one is called thrips) are tiny, skinny bugs less than a millimeter long. Mature thrips are usually brown or black. They multiply fast by laying eggs that are nearly impossible to see. Hatched babies, called nymphs, are white and look like adults, but smaller. Neem oil will kill them on contact. Saturate the entire plant and its soil.

DEALING WITH PESTS

Don't panic if you find pests on your succulents! They're easy to kill with everyday household products. I don't use harsh chemicals; they kill pests, but they aren't good for us or the environment. These are the products I use and recommend.

GENTLE DISH SOAP

Mix 1½ teaspoons of regular Dawn dish soap in a large (32-oz) plastic spray bottle filled with water. Completely drench the leaves and stems with this mild soap solution until every bug is washed away. The soap kills on contact, but the bugs can hide under leaves and stems. The soap mix can cover the plant and soil without causing any harm. It's best to pour some of the soap mix into the soil to kill bugs that might be hiding out. Let it sit for twenty minutes and rinse it off with water. This gentle soap solution is even safe for sensitive, rare succulents. Be sure to keep the plants in the shade. They are more sun-sensitive until the solution is rinsed off. Water plants again when the soil is dry.

If the bug infestation is heavy, it's a good idea to replace the soil. If you decide to do this, hold the plant over a wastebasket and carefully remove your plant from its container. Gently loosen the soil from around the roots, letting it fall away until the roots are bare. Once you've removed all the soil from the roots, make sure the roots are clear of pests by spraying them with Dawn dish soap solution and then rinsing the roots with cool water.

After the roots are clean, it's ready to repot with fresh soil. You don't necessarily need to throw out your container if you scrub it with Dawn dish soap and water. After you've washed it, it's safe to use.

ISOPROPYL ALCOHOL

Another way to kill pests is with 70 percent isopropyl alcohol, sold at grocery and drug stores in the first aid aisle. It also comes in stronger concentrations that are too harsh and can damage plants. If over 70 percent is all you can find, add a little water to dilute it down to 70 percent.

First, move your plant to a shady spot where it can stay for two to three days. 70 percent alcohol is safe to use on succulents, but the plant will die if it's left in the sun after treating it.

Pour the alcohol into a plastic spray bottle. I turn the nozzle to a medium spray setting and spray directly on the plant where I see signs of bugs. Be sure to look under the leaves and along the stems where leaves attach. They're common areas for pests to hide. You can even pour alcohol into the soil to kill any bugs in the soil and unhatched eggs. Alcohol kills most pests on contact. Alcohol can also be applied with a Q-tip. Dip the Q-tip in alcohol and clean away any sign of pests.

If your plant has a severe bug problem, it's best to replace the soil and scrub the container. Desoil the roots by gently loosening and removing all of the soil. It won't hurt your succulent to remove all the soil from its roots. Most succulents are shipped without soil (called bare root) or shipped as cuttings, without any roots at all.

Last, spray the roots with alcohol, and rinse them after a few minutes. Only reuse a pot after it's scrubbed well with soapy water. I use Dawn.

NEEM OIL

Neem is all-natural and great at killing pests. It comes from the fruit and seeds of neem trees. It doesn't harm ants, bees, ladybugs, earthworms, or even butterflies. It's environmentally friendly and is classified as an organic pesticide and fungicide safe for kitchen gardens.

In some countries, and by some people online, it's used to help various skin conditions and other ailments. I only use it on my plants. It doesn't sound unsafe to be around, but I'm still careful not to get it on me, and I wash my hands after spraying plants. Neem is absorbed into the plant, so it keeps working after it's dry. And it's very effective on every pest I've tried it on. It kills adult insects and their eggs.

You can find neem oil online and at most garden centers and nurseries.

Neem oil comes ready to spray or as a concentrate, so follow the instructions on the label to see if you need to dilute it. Most concentrated brands of neem have instructions to add water and mild dish soap, like Dawn.

Remember to keep your plant in a shady place for two to three days after treating, to prevent sunburn. The neem mixture will give your plants all the water they need until their soil dries. Repeat whenever you see pests. Some growers have found that using neem every three weeks prevents mealy and fungus caused by overwatering. I love how quickly neem works and how beautiful it makes my Hoyas look.

DIATOMACEOUS EARTH

Diatomaceous earth, often called DE, is a type of soil made from tiny, single-celled algae-like creatures called diatoms, which have glass-like shells. They live in water everywhere, but the diatoms in DE are fossils. They lived millions of years ago, and now form layers of a fine white powder-like chalk dust.

Food-grade DE is organic and nontoxic. There are even testimonials online from people who add it to a glass of water to drink as a food supplement. It's a broad-spectrum insect, snail, and slug killer, which means it kills both garden-friendly bugs and pests. It's so abrasive that it damages their exoskeleton when it gets on them, and they die from dehydration.

DE is also used in swimming pool filters to keep pool water clear. The DE for swimming pool filters has been heat-treated, and sometimes has had chlorine added—so it's best not to use pool-grade DE. Instead, use Food or garden grade available at hardware stores, garden centers, and online.

DE is harmless to touch. But it's very drying. The microscopic particles are sharp, so take care not to get it in your eyes or breathe in the dust. See the instructions on the container.

If you're worried about DE dust, it can be applied as a spray. Mix one part DE with three parts of water in a spray bottle and shake well. Spray it wherever you see bugs on or around your succulents, then pour some around the soil. The water evaporates, leaving a fine, even dusting of DE.

If you're careful about its dust, DE can be applied as a powder. An easy method is to use a small, dry squeeze bottle. You'll find them where you buy DE. I put DE in a two-inch plastic nursery pot (the ones you buy small plants in at Home Depot), and shake it gently to sprinkle the DE around the soil.

Sometimes I mix it into the soil of my potted plants. I don't use it in large areas of the garden because, although it won't kill earthworms, it does dehydrate good bugs, bees, and butterflies, and we need them in our gardens.

CINNAMON

Cinnamon is a natural fungicide. Dipping the end of succulents without well-established roots or bulbs (like String of Hearts bulbs) in cinnamon is amazingly effective at preventing fungus rot. It also helps to keep fungus from killing seeds as they germinate. This is an extra step that isn't done by everyone.

NATURAL PREDATORS

Ladybugs can help control garden pests. Buy ladybugs in the spring and early summer, before they lay all their eggs, and you'll have babies that eat more pests than the adults. If you buy them later in the summer, the adults will eat what they can find and then fly away, unless you buy packages of ladybug food. If you buy natural predators and still have a pest problem after setting them free in your yard, treating your plant with any other products will kill the ladybugs along with the pests.

FERTILIZING SUCCULENTS

FERTILIZER

Commercial fertilizer labels are standardized. They all have three bold numbers representing the main three nutrients in fertilizers. The numbers are always in this order: nitrogen (N), phosphorus (P), potassium (K). This is called the fertilizer grade, or NPK ratio.

When looking for fertilizer, you'll see that some labels have higher NPK numbers. Higher numbers mean the fertilizer is more potent. Succulents don't need strong fertilizer. Growing plants is a science, and there are different opinions and variables. Many professional succulent growers use a balanced fertilizer. The three NPK numbers match. Others have found another NPK formula works best for them. This is because of differences in local water and soil minerals. If you're new to growing succulents, try a mild NPK 5-5-5 formula and carefully follow the label's instructions.

An important thing to mention for more experienced succulent growers is that the fertilizer you apply washes away the next time you water your succulents. And the benefits can depend on how fast your soil dries and how often you water your plants. One of my favorite succulent growers uses a stronger fertilizer solution than other growers I know, and his plants are beautiful! Many are rare and considered very difficult to grow. He uses a higher strength because his greenhouse is warm and has constant airflow, so his soil dries very fast. The benefits of the fertilizer are soon washed away. It's always best to start with a very low concentration and see how your plants do.

WHEN TO FERTILIZE

Good cactus and succulent soils are full of nutrients, so it's not essential to fertilize when your soil is new. And with succulents, less is better. If you overdo, the nutrients can be toxic to succulents, attracting pests.

I fertilize in the spring when my succulents are actively growing. Follow the instructions on the fertilizer label carefully to dilute it correctly. Never apply fertilizer in full sun, or when the weather is hot—it can burn plants. Apply it early in the morning. If you're using granular fertilizer, make sure no solid granules are left on the leaves to burn them. Add the granular fertilizer on a day when you're watering your succulents. Never leave it on dry soil.

One of my expert succulent growers, who needs his plants to grow quickly, recommends adding fertilizer to the water for three weeks, then going three weeks without. He says this keeps the fertilizer from washing away the next time he waters.

SOIL pH

Dedicated succulent growers learn that slightly acidic soil helps roots absorb more nutrients. If your soil is alkaline, watering with slightly acidic water, with a pH of 5.5, can help balance the pH of the soil. A pH of 7 is considered neutral, pH under 7 is acidic, and pH over 7 is alkaline. If the soil pH is off, succulents won't necessarily die, but they'll grow slower. Testing water pH is easiest with pH test strips.

COFFEE GROUNDS

Some say that coffee or tea grounds can increase soil acidity. Still, it's not very effective because most of the acid goes into the drink. If you're looking to increase soil pH, white vinegar may work better. Add a little and test the pH of your water. If you don't have vinegar on hand, lemon works too.

Contact your local cactus and succulent society for more information and help on growing succulents in your area! You'll find friendly succulent experts willing to share their gardens and time with you.

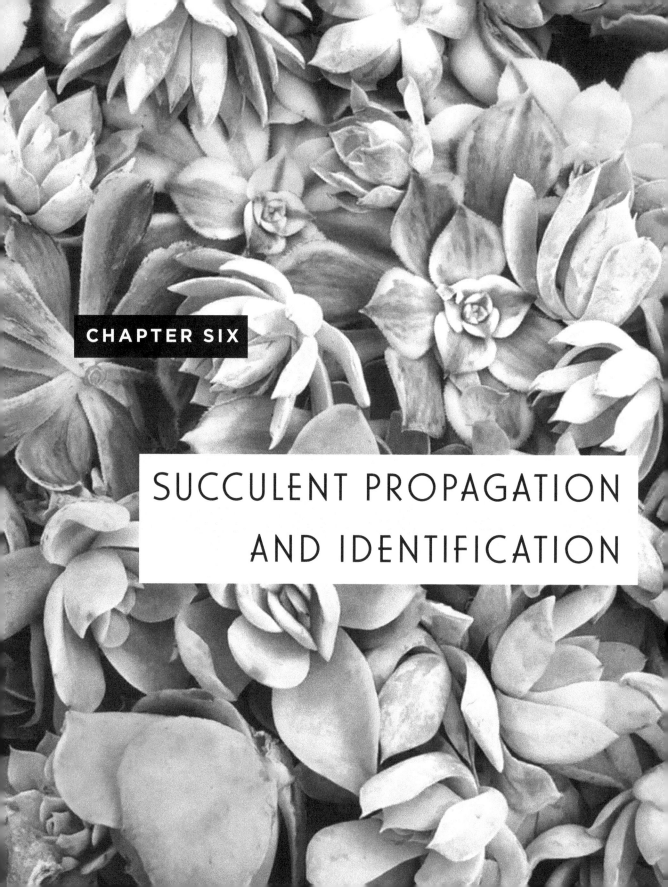

CHAPTER SIX

SUCCULENT PROPAGATION
AND IDENTIFICATION

Leaf babies in a heart shape. Photo by Fairyblooms.

GROWING SUCCULENT LEAF BABIES

Have you ever grown a new succulent from a single succulent leaf? They're fun to grow, and the tiny babies look like miniatures of their mother plant. I'll teach you some tricks to get nearly every leaf to grow.

The end of the leaf that attaches to the stem is slightly curved to match the stem; this end of the leaf is where a leaf baby will grow. Leaves nearest the roots are usually the easiest to remove.

Some succulents grow from cuttings but not from leaves. Haworthias, agave, most aeoniums, and sempervivums grow from cuttings, not leaves.

Occasionally a leaf will tear when you pull it from the stem. Most perfect leaves will grow leaf babies. But often, I'm surprised to see even torn leaves grow leaf babies, so I save all the leaves.

Professional succulent growers have different ways of starting leaf babies. Some set the leaves aside for several days to allow the leaf to heal over. Set your leaves aside in a shady place. I put mine on a garden flat, a plastic tray with a small lattice pattern of holes in the bottom. After the leaves have healed over, they tuck the ends of the leaves in damp succulent soil.

Other growers leave their succulent leaves on a garden flat and wait four to six weeks, until the leaf has roots and a tiny baby succulent has appeared, before setting the leaf on damp soil. The idea is to keep the leaf dry. Do not mist them or water them. After several weeks, small pink roots will start growing on the end of the leaf, where it was attached to the stem. During cool weather, it can take longer. A new baby succulent gets all the water and nutrients it needs to root from the mother leaf.

Leaf babies need to be grown close together or in a small space to grow well. Place the leaves in plug trays. Plug trays have many sections or cells about an inch across that hold soil. If the soil area is bigger, your leaf baby is less likely to survive.

If you're using plug trays, fill the plug tray sections with succulent soil (a mix of peat moss and perlite works well in my area). Dampen the soil, create a tiny dip, and set the leaf baby on the soil. If you don't have plug trays, leaf babies can share soil. Place leaf babies in small indents on damp soil about an inch apart.

Before the soil is dry, dampen it again, top to bottom. It's okay to get the mama leaf wet. Don't make the soil muddy. Damp soil holds its shape when it's clenched in the palm of the hand, without water dripping.

When the leaf babies are an inch across or have outgrown the plug tray, they can be moved to a larger pot. For best results, keep them in pots with no more than one to two inches of extra soil around them.

Experiment, try both ways of growing leaf babies to see which works best for you!

GROWING SUCCULENTS FROM CUTTINGS

Another way to grow succulents is by snipping the top of the plant off. It's called taking a cutting. Leave a row of leaves behind on the stem. New baby succulents will appear where the leaves grow on the stem. The cutting you took from the top of the plant will regrow new roots.

To propagate the cutting, set it aside, away from direct sunlight. The cut stem will heal, and after two or three weeks, tiny pink roots will begin to grow where the stem was cut. Once roots appear, your cutting is ready to be planted. If you set cuttings on soil before they have roots, don't water them. The leaves are full of water, and misting or watering the soil makes them more likely to rot before they sprout roots.

Choose a pot that's no more than twice the diameter of your succulent cutting. Fill it with dry cactus and succulent soil, then make a slight indent with your finger or a sharpened wooden dowel. Set the succulent cutting on the dry soil.

It's important not to water your plant for about another week while the roots grow strong enough to soak up water.

It's okay to pick your cutting up and check the roots. It won't slow its progress. It's alright if the leaves of your cutting become a little withered before it's time to water. If you water before the roots can soak up water, it can cause fungus rot. Once the roots are thriving, water the way you would a grown succulent.

WATER PROPAGATION

Water propagation isn't popular with commercial growers in the United States, but everyone should try it! It's easy and beautiful, and it's fun to watch the roots grow.

Take a cutting from a succulent plant. Set the cutting aside until the cut stem hardens or heals over. Succulent cuttings don't need roots to start water propagation.

I like to choose a clear glass jar to watch the beautiful roots grow. The top of the jar should be big enough to support the cutting as its small stem touches the water. Place the container on a windowsill or under fluorescent lights.

Your cutting is ready to plant when it has lots of thread-like roots. Or you can leave it in the water and watch it grow. To plant, choose a pot that's no more than half again the width of your cutting. Add a little dry cactus and succulent soil mix to the bottom of your pot. Prepare the roots by sprinkling them with cinnamon. This will help prevent fungus rot while your succulent is adjusting to absorbing water from the soil. Hold the plant in the pot and fill in the soil all around it. The soil should be high enough—close enough to the top of the planter—to allow easy airflow across the top of the soil.

Have you ever wondered why overwatered succulents often rot, but a succulent can sit in water for weeks or even months during water propagation? Yes! That's because it's not the water that's causing rot. It's a fungus that grows in soil, not water. If there's not plenty of air circulation, tiny fungus spores floating through the air can settle on wet soil. Some fungi can start to affect succulents in wet soil within three to four days. This is why I recommend that succulent soil be nearly dry within four days after watering.

GROWING SUCCULENTS FROM SEEDS

Dick Wright is a world-renowned succulent expert and plant breeder. I learned all about succulent seed propagation from him. Dick has developed hundreds of beautiful new succulent hybrids; I like to call them designer succulents. Most likely, some of your favorite succulents are among the ones he designed. These are a few you may know, Echeveria Tippy, Rain Drops, Moon Stones, and Echeveria Lola, a favorite hybrid of mine. Dick created it by cross-pollinating *Echeveria lilacina* and *Echeveria derenbergii*. And he named it for his sweet aunt Lola.

CROSS-POLLINATION

Cross-pollinating succulents is fun and exciting. Select two blooming succulents from similar families that you'd like to cross-pollinate. Use a small, clean paintbrush and gently brush the pollen from inside a blossom on the first plant and brush it inside a bloom on the second plant. Repeat with all the flowers on both plants. The pollen holds half of the plant DNA, and crossing it will combine the two plants to create your new succulent.

You may want to cover the bloom stocks with a bit of nylon stocking, so insects and hummingbirds don't do more cross-pollinating with other plants.

When the blooms and stalk are thoroughly dry and crispy, it's time to harvest the seeds. Cut the seed stalks off each plant with scissors and place them in a wide, shallow bowl. Strip the dried flowers from each stock by holding the stem firmly over the bowl and pulling the dried blossoms off through your fingers. You'll have tiny seeds and lots of dried petals in the bowl. It will look a bit like potpourri.

Use a metal kitchen strainer to separate the seeds from the dried bits of the bloom stalk. Set the stalks in the strainer and shake it over a dry bowl to catch the tiny seeds.

Gather the seeds and put them in a little paper envelope, never plastic, with the names of the succulents you got the bloom stalks from. This will keep the seeds and propagation information safe until you're ready to plant them.

Prepare a Container

An easy way to make a little seedling greenhouse is with a clear plastic disposable food container with a lid. Just put holes in the bottom for drainage. If you're growing many seeds, it's best to plant them in four-inch square pots set on a greenhouse flat. If a problem arises in one pot, like fungus, it doesn't affect all the plants.

Container Ventilation

Keep the seedlings covered. If you're using a plastic takeout food container, just close the lid. If you're using a greenhouse flat with four-inch pots, they can be covered with a piece of plexiglass.

If your plants are on the garden tray, the bottom has an open-weave pattern, and the pots have drainage, giving the little seedlings all the drainage needed.

Soil

Growing succulents is a science, so we're always learning. It's fun to test different soils. It's fascinating to visit Dick Wright's seed greenhouse and see a different soil mix being tested on each row of the same little seedlings.

Try your favorite succulent soil as a base and top it with a delicate covering of Miracle-Gro seedling mix. We use 50 percent peat or all-purpose potting soil and 50 percent perlite as our base soil.

Planting

Scatter the seeds on top of the soil as if you were salting food. Don't cover them. The seeds need light to germinate.

Watering

If you're able to collect rainwater, it's best for watering. Keep the soil damp. When it's barely moist, dampen it again using a spray bottle. Water enough for the soil to hold its shape when pressed in your hand. Keep it moist and covered until the seedlings come up.

Preventing Damping-Off (Seedling Fungus Rot)

Sterilize trays and pots in a solution of 10 percent household bleach and 90 percent water. Use new soil for seedlings. Also, make sure your seedling nursery has good drainage.

Temperature

The best temperature for seedlings is around 70 degrees. Bottom heat is essential for seedlings if it's colder than this in your area. A heat mat from a pet store works great! Just set it under your seedlings with a layer of perlite on top. They don't have temperature control, but they will keep the soil between 70 and 74 degrees.

Light

Seedlings need 50 percent sunlight, called filtered light or bright shade. Avoid direct sunlight.

Wait Time

Little seedlings will sprout in about two weeks. After two months, your seedling will be a tiny quarter-inch across and will grow fast throughout the growing season. Some grow faster than others.

Seedlings can be transferred into plug trays or individual two-inch pots when they are a quarter-inch across. Plug trays can be purchased online or at large garden centers. The grower must be careful to hold the seedlings by the leaves, never the stems.

Things to Watch Out for So Your Seedlings Will Thrive

The soil must stay damp and warm.

Take photos of the plant and its bloom once your new seedling has matured and flowers. This will help you compare it with similar succulents to see whether you've developed a new hybrid! You can submit your request to register your plant along with photos and the names of the succulents you used for cross-pollination. Include your name and the name you'd like the hybrid to be called.

SECTION III

CRAFTS

CHAPTER SEVEN

EVENTS AND WEDDINGS
TO REMEMBER

TABLETOP SUCCULENT GARLAND

A succulent garland makes an exquisite table decoration for a wedding or elegant party. And they're easy to make—I'll show you how.

Greenery can be found locally or at a flower market. I like to gather mine locally. Look in your area for trees or vines with closely spaced, beautifully shaped leaves. All the same or a mix of greenery are equally beautiful.

I don't recommend using moss instead of greenery. It can look messy, and without a container, little bits of moss from the table can end up on clothing and food.

Gather the greenery into little bundles. The size of the bundle depends on how delicate or full you'd like the garland to be. Keep the stems long for now; you'll cut them when you see the best length. Stagger the length at the top of the bundle slightly to look natural. Wire the stems in the bundle together with 26-gauge florist paddle wire. Make a second bundle similar to the first.

Set the first bundle on a table and lay the second over it about halfway down, where the leaves begin to thin or where it will look like it's part of the first bundle. Wire the bundles together. Repeat this until you have the length you'd like for your table.

Add succulent cuttings to your garland. Make sure you cut your succulent stems so that you have about a half-inch to wire the succulent. Use 20-gauge wire. Push the wire through the stem. Push the succulent onto the wire about four inches, then bend the wire down close to the stem.

Use waxed florist tape to wrap the stem. Start close to the succulent leaves and wrap it down the wire about four inches. Cut the extra wire. Repeat with all of the cuttings you'll be using in the garland.

Wrap the wired succulent stem onto the garland, spaced about evenly or with some in small groups of two or three.

CARE

The greenery will stay fresh if kept cool and in the shade for only a couple of days, so set aside time before your event.

FORMAL SUCCULENT TABLETOP ARRANGEMENTS

If you choose a container for a dinner party or an event, height often adds elegance. But if the arrangement is for a dinner table, remember that it's nice to see the person you're sitting across from. A low-profile arrangement, up to eighteen inches tall, won't block anyone's view. But if your heart is set on a taller container, make sure it has a narrow stem that's tall enough for the arrangement to be above head level. Choose tall containers carefully. A broad, sturdy base is essential to keep your planter stable when the table is jiggled, or the wind blows. It's memorable, if not disastrous, to have your tall arrangement fall into someone's lap!

Your container doesn't need soil. The succulents will look beautiful for several weeks and can be cut from their wired stems and planted after your event. Directions: Thread a 20 gauge wire through the stem of each succulent cutting. Fold the wire down on either side of the stem. Wrap the wire stem from top to bottom with waxed floral tape. A brick of styrofoam or floral foam will hold the wired succulent stems in place. Trailing succulents do not need to be wired, just tuck them in beside the floral foam.

SUCCULENT-TRIMMED WEDDING ARCH

Designing a succulent trimmed wedding arch is similar to making a succulent garland. The arch will be bigger and seen from a distance, so use more greenery and larger, six-inch succulents with the four-inch succulents. Larger succulents take a thicker, 18-gauge wire to hold heavier succulent cuttings in place. Use one-inch waxed floral tape instead of half-inch.

An arch doesn't need to be covered with a garland. A section of garland across the top and/or a floral spray on each side is beautiful.

SUCCULENT CAKE TOPPER

A succulent-topped cake complements any wedding style beautifully! And with so many succulents to choose from, you're sure to find colors to match your color theme.

If you've chosen a baker for your wedding cake, skip down four paragraphs to *Adding a Succulent Cake Topper*.

If you're planning a wedding with a limited budget, saving on your wedding cake can make a big difference. To create this wedding cake on a budget, order three birthday cakes from a grocery store bakery, a ten-inch, an eight-inch, and a five-inch mini. Ask for cakes that are lightly frosted with white buttercream frosting. This style is often called a naked cake. Show the baker a photo to really convey the look you want for the frosting. Before you finalize the order, try a cupcake in your cake choice to make sure you like it.

It's easiest if you don't add extra fruit or fancy fillings. If the baker will agree to cut the cardboard base so it won't show under the cake, have them do it. If they will not, you can cut it yourself. Ask for the cakes to be cold when you pick them up. Cold cakes are easier to stack.

It's best to insert plastic cake dowels, available at craft stores and online, to support a three-tiered cake. To measure the correct length for the dowels, push a cake dowel into the ten-inch cake, three inches in from the edge. Mark the height of the cake on the plastic dowel with a pencil. Pull out the dowel—twist it as you pull to remove it easily. Cut the dowel with a sprinkler-pipe cutter at the pencil mark. Next, cut three more pieces the same length. Reinsert the plastic cake dowel in the hole and add the remaining three to make a square three inches in from the edge of the cake.

Do the same for the eight-inch middle layer. This time, push in the dowel 3.5 inches from the outer edge of the cake. Mark the height of the cake on the plastic cake dowel with a pencil. Remove the dowel and cut it at the pencil mark. Cut three more plastic cake dowels the same length. Insert the four plastic cake dowels as before, but 2.5 inches in from the outer edge of the cake. Your cakes are ready to stack.

Two eight-inch grocery store cakes can also be stacked beautifully. Some grocery stores don't offer a ten-inch cake. Add the plastic dowels an inch in from the side of the bottom layer. Lift the cake with a stainless-steel cake lifter shovel available online and at baking and craft stores.

STACKING THE CAKE LAYERS

Mark the frosting on top of the ten-inch cake with a toothpick two inches in from the edge in four places. Set the eight-inch cake in place, using the marks as a guide.

Mark the frosting on top of the eight-inch cake with a toothpick 1.5 inches in from the edge in four places. Lift the top (five-inch) layer and set it on the eight-inch cake, lining up the edges with the marks on the cake frosting. Icing repair is easy with a non-serrated knife blade dipped in water. You're ready to trim your cake with succulents!

ADDING A SUCCULENT CAKE TOPPER

Succulent cuttings can be dunked in a solution of ½ cup bleach and 5 cups water to sanitize them, then rinse with clear water.

Choose eight to twelve succulents of various sizes to create your cake topper.

Leave a short stem when cutting the succulent stems.

Thread floral wire through the stem, and bend it down over the stem.

Use floral tape and wrap four inches down the wire stem.

Succulent cuttings (never succulents with roots) can be sanitized safely in a solution of one part bleach and ten parts water. Dip the succulent in the mild bleach solution for ten to twenty seconds, rinse in cool water, and set on a paper towel.

Plan where you'd like to put the succulents, so they won't need to be moved after putting the wire stems in the cake. If you do mess up the cake frosting a bit, run a smooth knife (without a serrated edge) under warm water and gently repair the frosting with the damp knife blade.

SUCCULENT GUEST FAVORS

Choose small containers for your party favors. Mini terra cotta pots, tin buckets, or small glasses are a few things to look for.

Two- to 2.5-inch succulents are a perfect size for party favors.

Take the succulents out of their little plastic garden pots and leave the soil on. Wrap moss around the soil and put the plant with the moss into the little planter. You may need to use a metal straw around the outside edge of the moss to help push the succulent into the pot.

CARE

Bright morning or late afternoon sunlight keeps succulents colorful. No need to water for a week or two. A simple test to see if they need water is to cup your fingers around the leaves of one of the succulents, press them together, and release them. If the leaves spring back, they don't need water. If they feel leathery as you bundle them and they slowly reopen after pressing them together, they are dry. Add two tablespoons of water. It's easy to water these small favors with a large medicine dropper or syringe (often used to measure children's medicines).

SUCCULENT BOUTONNIERE

Choose three small (two-inch) succulent rosettes. These are symmetrical succulents with petal-shaped leaves that make them look like flowers. Look for echeveria and sedum succulents, and one small, upright, branching crassula succulent like baby necklace, rupestris, or brevifolia.

Leave a small stem on the cuttings.

Push a floral wire through the rosette stem, then bend it down over the stem.

Set a wire beside the stem of the crassula. Several leaves on the stem often need to be removed before wrapping the stem.

With floral tape, start at the top of the stem and wrap one inch down the wired stem.

Leave the wire bare for the last three inches.

Prepare each of the four succulents with wire and floral tape.

Choose two succulents and hold their stems together, with one succulent slightly higher than the second. Wrap the two stems together with floral tape, starting at the top, and wrap one inch down.

Add the third succulent to the little arrangement. Wrap floral tape around the stems, top to bottom.

Add the crassula behind the three little succulents and wrap floral tape around all the stems, top to bottom.

Curl the stems around a metal straw or a pencil, making about three twists.

Trim the curled tip with wire cutters so all the wire ends are the same length.

Tie with a ribbon or wrap with a double strand of thin hemp twine and tie a bow (hemp is a smoother twine that keeps its shape in the rain).

CARE

Bright morning or late afternoon sunlight keeps succulents colorful. No need to water for a week or two. These little succulents can be cut from their metal stems, and they'll regrow roots like all succulent cuttings. See more information on growing succulent cuttings on page 164.

SUCCULENT WRIST CORSAGE

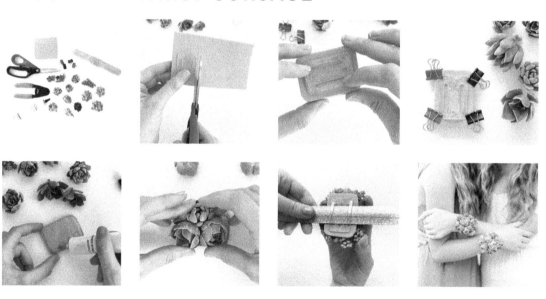

Begin with any bracelet to decorate with succulents. I prefer florist slap bracelets because one size fits all, and they fit snugly yet comfortably. A snug bracelet is important. Succulents are heavy from water stored in their leaves, and they'll slide under the wrist if the bracelet is too loose.

Use skin-colored craft foam available at craft stores or online. They come in twelve-by-eighteen-inch sheets. Use the 5mm thickness. Next, cut the foam to the size and shape you'd like. The succulents will go a bit beyond the edges. Lay the bracelet flat and remove the sliding corsage base. Next, apply floral adhesive to the slider. Press the foam to the slider to attach it. Use metal office clamps while the glue dries.

While the adhesive is drying, which takes about five minutes, use scissors to cut succulent stems flat from the base of the leaves. Remove the clamps. Apply floral adhesive to the bottom of the trimmed piece of foam. While it's drying, set out your succulent design next to it. Begin with the center of the design, adding succulents one at a time with floral adhesive on the bottom of each plant. Avoid touching the center stem with wet adhesive. Add baby plants to fill in any tiny gaps. After about five to ten minutes, everything will be dry. That's it!

CARE

Bright shade or morning sunlight can keep your succulent wrist corsage colorful. There's no need to water for a week or two, maybe more, depending on the humidity. Tiny roots will grow, and the stem will heal over. If their little plump leaves start looking limp after two weeks, they can have water. Remove the sliding craft foam base from the bracelet and dip it in cool water for about twenty seconds. Set it on a paper towel to dry. With water and bright shade, your wrist corsage can stay looking fresh and beautiful for months.

SUCCULENT COMB

Choose a hair comb that won't be damaged by water. You'll also need some office clips, scissors, floral adhesive, and a 2mm-thick sheet of craft foam.

Place the edge of the craft foam on the solid edge of the comb. Cut the foam a half-inch wider on each side, beyond the edge of the comb. Bend the foam at the top edge of the comb and fold it over to cover both sides. Add clips to each side of the comb, then trim the foam to fit the top area of the comb.

Next, glue the foam to the top and bottom of the comb. Be very careful that no glue gets on the teeth of the comb. Add clips to each side of the foam and let it completely dry. Once it's dry, trim the edges of the foam to the comb.

After the foam is attached to the comb, apply floral adhesive to attach the succulents. Wait a minute for the glue to thicken and become tacky. While the glue on the comb is drying, lay out the plants next to it in the design you'll be using. Begin adding plants from the center outward. Use glue on the bottom of the leaves, avoiding the center stem. Use larger plants first, then fill empty spots with baby cuttings until the foam is completely covered.

CARE

Bright morning or late afternoon sunlight will keep your succulent comb looking vibrant. There's no need to water for a week or two, maybe more, depending on the humidity. Tiny roots will grow along the stems, unseen between the succulents, and the stems will heal over. If the small plump leaves start looking limp after two weeks, dip the comb in cool water for about twenty seconds, then leave it to dry. Sunlight and watering once or twice a week as needed can keep the succulents looking fresh for months.

SUCCULENT CROWN

What you'll need: two eighteen-inch lengths of 18-gauge floral wire to create the crown base, also 22- or 24-gauge floral wire to wire the small succulents to be cut in four-inch lengths, 2½-inch or less succulent cuttings, jewelry pliers with a flat or needle nose, tin snips or wire cutter, half-inch wax-covered floral tape, and ribbon or hemp twine. If you'd like, you can add dried florals such as baby's breath, lavender, pepper berries, tallow berries, etc.

Measure around the head and determine how many inches of succulents will be used. Add four or more inches to that measurement. If the length you've decided on is more than eighteen inches, you'll need to stagger the two wires for the full measurement.

Take the two 18-gauge wires and join them together with the floral tape, wrapping with a slight twist as you go. Next, you'll make a slight bend in the joined wires. It's easy to bend them above your knee. This will form the crown's base.

Gather succulent cuttings you'll need for the crown. I use a variety of mostly echeveria and sedum rosettes, symmetrical plants in the shape of a flower bloom. I like to add smaller crassula plants with hardy stems like baby's necklace. Succulent cuttings should range in size from a little less than two inches for the largest down to about a half-inch for the smallest.

Each cutting needs a quarter-inch stem. With the 22- or 24-gauge wire lengths, push the wire through a succulent stem and thread it to the midway point of the wire. Then bend the wire, doubling it down along the stem of the succulent cutting. With floral tape, begin directly beneath the plant stem and tightly wrap the plant to the joined wires, twisting and slightly stretching as you go. Wrap until covered.

Next, begin adding the wrapped succulents one by one to the crown base. Start with small crassulas or dried florals at one end of the crown base. The plants will point toward the end of the base. Continue toward the center of the crown. Depending on size, each plant will be approximately a quarter- to a half-inch apart. Use gradually larger plants until the center is reached with the largest plant. Once the largest plant is in place, continue to the opposite end with plants descending in size. You'll want the two sides to balance symmetrically.

Use the flat-nosed pliers to bend the wire end of the crown, creating a loop on each end. Secure the loops with half-inch waxed floral tape. Use a length of ribbon or twine, fold it in half, and thread the folded end through the loop. Hold the folded end, thread the two loose ends through the fold, and pull.

SUCCULENT WEDDING BOUQUET

What you'll need: 18-gauge floral wire in eighteen-inch lengths. This is sold in bundles at craft stores and online. One-inch and half-inch waxed floral tape, tin snips, hemp twine or ribbon, and succulent cuttings ranging from two to four inches. Your succulent cuttings need half-inch stems. You'll also need a heavy vase that's about eight inches tall.

As you work with the succulents, touch their leaves as little as possible so you won't leave fingerprints in their fine powdery coating.

Each cutting will need to have a wire stem. To wire a succulent, push the wire through the stem about four inches. Bend the wire down along the stem. The wire needs to lie against the stem, with no gaps.

Use half-inch waxed floral tape and wrap it around the wire stem. Start the tape directly under the succulent leaves. The waxed tape will stick to itself as it's wrapped. Stretch it slightly as you wrap. I've found it's easiest to hold the succulent by its stem with my left hand, the waxed tape in my right. I roll the stem between my fingers to turn the stem while positioning the tape and wrapping it with my right hand. Wrap the tape all the way to the bottom.

Wire all the cuttings for the bouquet. I keep them looking nice by placing them in a vase as they're wired instead of laying them on a table.

Building the bouquet:

Select two succulents you'd like for the top of the bouquet. Position them with their stems together. Use the half-inch floral tape to wrap the stems together. Start a few inches below the succulents and wrap to the bottom of the stems.

Wrap the stems together with waxed floral tape after adding each succulent as you build the bouquet. Start bending the wire, so the succulents face out instead of upward, when the top of the bouquet is the width you want it to be. Keep the succulents close together. The last row of stems should be pointing outward at a right angle. Wire stems should never be seen unless the bouquet is upside down.

When all the succulents are in place, wrap around the stems several times with one-inch waxed floral tape to give them a smooth look and feel. Also, use waxed tape to cover the bottom of the stems.

Put the finishing touches on your bouquet. I'll teach you two techniques that will help you to personalize your bouquet stem.

The twine wrap can be used with any thin cord or ribbon. Set aside two feet of extra twine at the top of the stem. Bring the remaining twine down along the stem and wrap the stem from the bottom up. You'll be covering the twine you brought down along the stem as you wrap the stems. When you're two inches from the top, lower the two feet of extra twine you set aside and continue wrapping above it until all of the green stem of the bouquet is covered.

Gather the two ends of twine to tie a bow. I add a second piece of twine when I tie the two ends to make a double bow.

A ribbon wrap is similar to the twine wrap. Start at the bottom and wrap the ribbon up the stem. When you reach the top, fold the end under and pin it in place with two or three pixie bouquet pins. They're about an inch long and come with a ball-shaped metal or pearl-colored head.

CARE

Before the Wedding

Your succulent bouquet requires nothing but sunshine before your wedding day. Bright, indirect sunshine will bring out the succulent's beautiful colors. Avoid summer midday sun. It will burn their leaves. Please protect from frost.

After the Wedding

Within two weeks after your wedding, cut each succulent from its wired stem. Follow instructions for growing succulents from cuttings on page 142.

CHAPTER EIGHT

SEASONS AND HOLIDAYS

SUCCULENT BIRDHOUSE

For this project, you'll need a wooden birdhouse. Look for one with a hinged bottom or back for easy cleaning each year—this will encourage birds to use it again. I look for unique little twigs when I'm on a walk or at the park to use for a perch. The mesh I use to cover the moss is garden bird netting mesh, used to protect kitchen gardens from birds. You'll need long-strand sphagnum moss, available at craft stores and online. You'll need an upholstery staple gun, floral adhesive, floral fern pins, 20-gauge florist wire, and flat-nosed pliers. If you're adding a twig for the perch, you'll need to drill a hole in the birdhouse for it. Before you start, add hardware for hanging your birdhouse.

Lay the mesh over the roof to see how much your birdhouse will need. Add six inches to the length for the raw edges to be turned under the roof. Cut the mesh to size. Open it up to double the width you'd like to plant. Lay the moss on one side of the mesh and roll it up in the mesh, like a sausage.

Set the mesh on the roof and use the staple gun to attach it under the roof on each side. Be sure to turn the edges under. Add staples to the mesh on the top of the roof so the moss stays in place.

Start with large succulents at the top of the roof. Poke a hole in the moss with pliers. Thread a wire through the succulent stem and set the stem in the hole you've made in the moss. Wrap the wire around the sausage and twist it in the back to secure the succulent in place. Use fern pins for medium-sized plants or where it's challenging to maneuver the wire. Use floral adhesive for small plants to fill in empty spaces. Be creative! Use some fun and unusual succulents.

GRAPEVINE WREATH TRIMMED WITH SUCCULENTS

Grapevine wreaths come in all sizes. They're sold at craft stores and online. My favorites are heart-shaped and circular. To make a grapevine wreath trimmed with succulents, choose your grapevine wreath and the number of succulent cuttings you'd like to add to it. I use four-inch succulents when making a wreath that's twelve inches or larger, and two- to three-inch plants to fill any small open areas the larger succulents don't cover. You'll need long-strand sphagnum moss, flat-nosed pliers, a paddle of 24-gauge floral wire, and eighteen-inch lengths of 20-gauge wire. The wire is sold at craft and floral supply stores and online. Sometimes I use floral adhesive when adding smaller plants to fill in after larger succulents are in place.

Set moss on the part of the wreath you'd like to plant. The moss should be thick enough that you can't feel the grapevine beneath it. The succulent cuttings grow roots into the moss.

Start on one end of the moss. Start the paddle wire off with a three-inch tail. You'll need it to tie off the end of the wire. Wrap the wire around the mossed area twice from one end to the other. Keep the wire tight as you wrap. Twist the two ends together to keep the wire tight.

Choose your first succulent, push a 22-gauge wire through the stem, and thread it halfway down the wire. Start your design in the middle of the mossed area. Wrap the wire around the wreath, so the succulent is anchored against it. Twist the wire at the back and tuck it under. Using the flat-nosed pliers makes getting a tight twist easier.

Add more wired succulents on each side of the first one until you reach the ends of the moss. I fit smaller succulents in wherever I see spaces, and some near the ends of the mossed area.

CARE

Succulents like long hours of bright light, but most cannot tolerate the intense, direct sunlight during hot summer months. They like to dry out between waterings, so watch the moss and only water when it's dry. Soaking your wreath in cool water for about twenty minutes once a week to once every other week, when the moss is completely dry, is usually enough.

If the stems of your succulents start growing long with a space between their petals, they are stretching for more light. If the succulents fade or turn pale, they need more light.

SUCCULENT-TRIMMED PUMPKINS

Real pumpkins are fun to trim with succulents, but they don't last long. A faux pumpkin stays beautiful! Craft stores have all sizes of faux pumpkins in the fall, and they're perfect for trimming with succulents. If you're looking for an autumn centerpiece or placeholders for a special fall get-together, this is the one!

Real pumpkins don't need soil, or a planting area cut into the pumpkin, to plant them with succulents. Succulents grow beautifully in moss.

If you're using a faux pumpkin, begin by spraying it lightly with a clear, matte sealer. After the sealer is dry, use fern pins to secure the moss to the top of the pumpkin. Add a little floral adhesive along the edges to add delicate, trailing moss. If you can't find floral adhesive, an acid-free, waterproof glue works well.

Create a pretty arrangement with the four-inch succulent cuttings in the center of the moss. They can be anchored to the moss with fern pins. Push the fern pin in around a leaf or through the stem. I add smaller succulent cuttings around the center arrangement and secure them with fern pins. Use two-inch and smaller cuttings to fill in on the edges. String of Beads (a.k.a. String of Pearls) can be added with fern pins to cascade down a side of the pumpkin. Use adhesives on the backs of the leaves and not the stems of fresh cuttings.

SEMPERVIVUM WREATH

Sempervivums are some of the most beautiful yet hardy succulents around. They grow easily in the Alps, despite extreme heat in summer and cold, snowy winters. That's how they got their name, sempervivum, which means "always or forever living." My first sempervivum wreath was made as a special request for a wreath that could withstand cold winters.

Sempervivums grow in clumps with little offshoots that spread over an area. Leave them in a planter long enough, and they'll creep adorably over the edge. They're constantly growing, with new babies taking the place of mama plants that have bloomed and die.

Sempervivum wreaths are a gorgeous patchwork of greens, reds, purples, and lavenders.

Make the moss wreath form with the step-by-step guide on page xx or find a moss wreath at garden centers or online.

Sempervivums have colors and patterns that go beautifully together, so they look charming planted in patches of the same variety. Select five or six sempervivum varieties. Some of my favorites are Pacific Blue Ice, Ruby Heart, Bronco, Arachnoideum Cobweb, Royal Ruby, Downland Queen, Arenaria... I don't know where to stop. I guess I love them all!

Some sempervivums have thick, dense stems and can be anchored to a wreath by pushing a 20-gauge floral wire through the stem, wrapping the wire around the wreath, and twisting the back to secure it. Others can be anchored to the moss wreath with floral fern pins. Plant larger sempervivums, like Pacific Blue Ice, alone between the patches of smaller ones.

SUCCULENT-TRIMMED HOLIDAY GRAPEVINE TREE

Cone-shaped grapevine is just the right shape for a holiday tree.

Press the moss into a ribbon shape. Add floral adhesive or acid-free glue under the moss tree, using moss and 24-gauge paddle wire around the tree to secure the moss. The paddle wire nestles into the grapevine, so it's barely visible.

Use one- to three-inch succulent cuttings to trim the tree.

Leave about a half-inch stem on the larger cuttings. Push a fine 22- or 24-gauge wire through the stem of a little two-inch succulent.

Start by adding succulent cuttings at the top of the tree.

Put the succulent against the moss a few inches from the top, wrap the wire around the tree, and twist it to secure it in place.

You'll be anchoring a few succulent cuttings every four to five inches. The rest of the succulents can be added with floral adhesive around the stems. Avoid putting glue directly on the freshly cut stems. The succulents that are wired will help to support the others.

Add smaller succulents with floral adhesive up to the top of the tree and gradually larger succulents toward the bottom of the tree.

SUCCULENT CHRISTMAS TREE ORNAMENTS

A small hanging glass terrarium will sparkle with the lights on the tree. Glass terrariums come in teardrop or round shapes of all sizes. They're sold at hobby and craft stores and online.

Add a little patch of moss to the bottom and create a mini arrangement with succulent cuttings, or add just one succulent cutting. Tie the top with a holiday ribbon and hang it on the tree.

A tillandsia air plant can be put in a hanging terrarium without moss or soil. Just tie a festive ribbon at the top and hang it on the tree.

HEART-SHAPED GRAPEVINE TRIMMED WITH SUCCULENTS

Grapevine is easy to shape after it's soaked in water for a few days. Make a heart from a round grapevine wreath by soaking it until the grapevine is soft and pliable. This takes two or three days. Bend the bottom together, so it comes to a point. Wrap two strong zip ties on each side near the bottom, then pull the two sides together with a third zip tie between them.

Cut through the top of the wreath with pruning shears. Bend the two sides down to a point. Use zip ties to hold the two ends together. Put the grapevine on the ground with something heavy on top to keep it from curling while it dries. Before you take the zip ties off, bind the top together by wrapping with 18-gauge wire three or four times. Trim the extra wire behind the wreath and tuck it into the grapevine, so no sharp ends are sticking out.

Put long-strand sphagnum moss on the left side of the wreath. I like to use the preserved green color. Use succulent cuttings to trim the wreath. Each cutting should be cut to have a half-inch stem. Push a 20-gauge wire through the stem and thread it halfway onto the wire.

Put this first wired succulent cutting on the wreath where the side of the heart arches toward the middle. Add two more to make a pretty arrangement, then work down the side of the moss, adding wired succulents. Watch to see that they aren't all in a row, stagger them a bit, and use some smaller than others.

Use smaller succulents toward the ends of the mossed area at the bottom and top. If there are any spaces between the succulents, filler succulents like pink jellybeans or crassula can easily be added with floral adhesive.

CARE

Wait at least two weeks for the succulent cuttings to harden or heal over where they were cut before watering your wreath. This will give little roots time to begin to grow. Hang your wreath where it will have full early morning or later afternoon sunshine. Bright shade on the edge of sunlight will keep your succulents bright and compact.

Blue and green succulents need less sunlight, so if the area only has indirect sunlight or bright shade part of the day, choose blue or green succulents.

Dip the succulent side of your wreath in cool water when the moss is completely dry. Unless the temperature is over eighty degrees, this is usually only once a week in summer. Protect from frost.

CHAPTER NINE

PERSONAL AND HOME DÉCOR

SUCCULENT RING

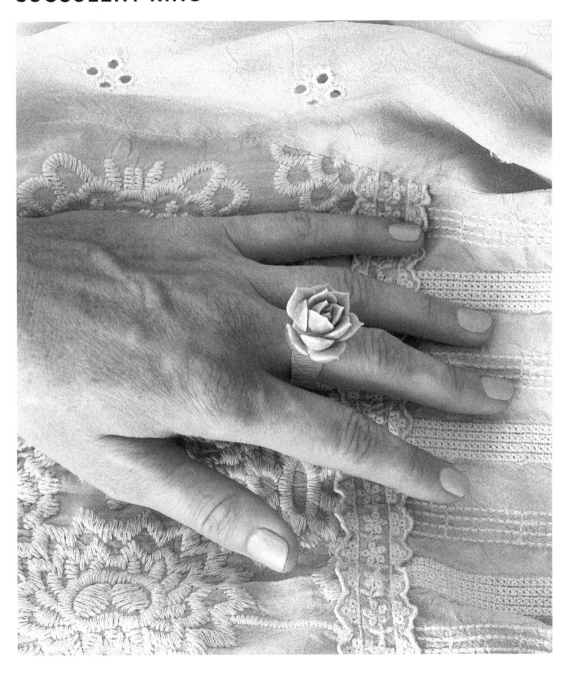

Have you ever wanted to wear a succulent? Now you easily can. Select a ring that's finger width, with a top to put the succulent on.

Add floral adhesive to the top of the ring directly where the little succulent will be placed.

Choose a small succulent and cut the stem off flat against the leaves.

Put floral adhesive around the leaves, avoiding the stem of the freshly cut succulent.

Wait for a minute for the adhesive on the ring and the succulent to become tacky instead of wet.

Press the succulent gently onto the ring and enjoy!

CARE

Set your ring on a windowsill with bright but not direct sunlight. After two weeks, dip in water once a week to help to keep it fresh.

SUCCULENT BODY ART

This is a fun project! And it's comfortable and secure to wear morning until night. Beautiful on a shoulder or arm, or around an ankle.

What you'll need: small succulent cuttings with no stem, KT tape, Oasis Floral Adhesive, and scissors. KT (kinesiology tape) sticks securely to the skin, and when it's time to take it off, it's painless to remove. Choose skin-colored tape, so any little bit of KT tape that might show won't be noticeable. KT tape is available at drug stores and online. It comes in neon and bright colors, so notice the color before you buy.

Without removing the backing, lay the tape on your shoulder or wherever you'd like to wear it. Mark a small dot with a sharpie pen where you'd like the focal point of your design. The dot may be closer to one end of the tape than the other. If the KT tape is longer than the design, mark where it will be cut.

Cut the tape to any shape you'd like your design to have. Or you can cut around the succulents when they're in place. If you think you'll alter the design shape as you go, cut the KT tape after the succulents are in place. Doing it later is more challenging.

Design your succulent arrangement and set it beside the KT tape. If the tape will curve over a shoulder, ankle, or arm, make the design longer than the tape and add it with the tape curved to avoid gaps when the tape bends.

Next, smooth floral adhesive to cover the top of the KT tape. While the adhesive dries to tacky, add it to the backs of the succulent cuttings, avoiding the freshly cut stems. Place each succulent, adhesive side up, back into its place in the design layout.

KT tape will stay in place until it's painlessly removed. It may stick a second time, but the tape loses stickiness after being removed. The cuttings are too fragile to sleep in, so this body art is for a special occasion. The cuttings can be gently removed from the tape, set in bright shade until they grow roots, and then set on succulent or cactus soil to grow.

SUCCULENT HEADBAND

Choose small succulent cuttings with a flat stem for your headband. Cuttings under two inches across are best.

Put floral adhesive on the headband only where you will be adding succulent cuttings. Set the headband aside.

Cut the stems off flat against the bottom leaves of the plant.

Set the succulent cuttings beside the headband in the design you'd like.

Add floral adhesive around the bottom leaves of each cutting, avoiding the newly cut stem, and turn them carefully upside down.

Gently press each succulent in place on the headband, starting in the middle with the larger of the small plants. Work your way to each end of the glued headband.

CARE

A succulent headband can stay beautiful for several weeks, kept in a bright shade. Wait two weeks before dipping in water to keep the succulent cuttings fresh. After two weeks, if the headband can be dipped in water several times a week, it will look beautiful longer.

SUCCULENT HAT BAND

Select succulents that are under three inches. Cut their stems off flat against their leaves. Plan and lay out your design beside the visor or hat. Next, add floral adhesive to the visor or hatband only where you'll add succulent cuttings. Add Oasis Floral Adhesive carefully; it does not dry clear. Next, apply the floral adhesive to the bottom of the succulent leaves, around—not on—the freshly cut stems. Gently press the succulents into place. If you'd like a removable hatband, read on for more details.

Craft foam can be used to make a removable hatband. Cut 5mm craft foam to the length and twice the height you'd like for your design.

Add floral adhesive along the top and bottom of the craft foam near the edge (do not glue the length, only the top, and bottom). Let it sit for a minute, then press it together for a permanent seal. I don't join the sides to look seamless because the seam helps the foam lay flat against the hat.

Plan and lay out your design beside the foam. Spread floral adhesive on one side of the foam and set it aside while you add glue to the bottom of the succulent cuttings. Avoid getting adhesive on freshly cut stems. Set them back beside the sliding base, upside down.

Gently press the succulents onto the foam.

Cut a piece of stretch fabric to size. Leave extra fabric to join the ends with a knot or zip tie. Slide the foam onto one end of the fabric (a thin wooden dowel can push it through easily). Tie a knot or use a zip tie to secure the ends of the fabric, then slide the succulents to cover the knot or zip tie.

SUCCULENT RIBBON DOG COLLARS

Dressing up your pups with succulent-trimmed ribbon "collars" adds a fun dash of style to k-9 guests . But be sure to watch your pet, even if you use pet-safe succulents like echeveria, sedum, and sempervivum, to prevent choking hazards and toxicity from eating the adhesive.

Select a ribbon that's about two inches wide. Be sure to get enough ribbon to tie in a bow, or add Velcro on the ends.

Select small succulents up to two inches across for your design. Cut the stems off flat against the bottom of the succulent leaves.

Spread floral adhesive on the ribbon where you'll add the succulents. Set the ribbon aside for the floral adhesive to dry enough to become tacky.

Add floral adhesive to the back of each succulent cutting, avoiding the freshly cut stems. Turn each cutting glue side up and set it back in place beside the ribbon.

Place your design on the ribbon, adding the center succulents first, then work outwards. The floral adhesive will be very sticky!

Be sure that the adhesive is completely dry before tying the ribbon onto your dog!

CARE

Succulent cuttings will keep looking beautiful for several weeks with indirect sunlight. Remove the succulents carefully from the sash to regrow them as cuttings. See details on growing succulents from cuttings on page 142.

ACKNOWLEDGMENTS

I'd like to thank the wonderful, inspiring people who have worked with me and contributed their time and talents to help me with this book: My loving husband, Scott, encouraged and patiently worked beside me, shouldering many day-to-day responsibilities of running our small business, Succulent Artworks, while I was busy writing. Angelique Howard, our daughter and owner of Fairyblooms. I also want to thank Mike Pyle, Jim Bishop, Dianne Reese, and Dick Wright. Also, our amazing Succulent Artworks team, Tyra Kobriger, Charity Davidson, Marcy Doumit, Noelle Buffet, and Marlene Walder. And our dear succulent growers who have become friends and mentors.

P.S.

Thanks for reading! I sincerely hope that you have enjoyed this book, and that the projects and techniques spark your imagination and elevate your succulent designs. Please reach out to me with questions or ideas on your design projects. You have a standing invite to email me (julia@succulentartworks.com). I would like to make learning and creativity as interactive as possible. Along those lines, please visit me @ SucculentArtworks to connect on Instagram and other social media. I'm constantly posting ideas and photos. Gardening is an art and a science. We're all continually learning new things. Please share!

I welcome all reader feedback. If you like the book, please let me know and post a review on Amazon. If you didn't like it, well, don't forget what your mother once told you, "If you can't say something nice…"

Wishing you happy days and sunshine!

Julia

ABOUT THE AUTHOR

Julia Hillier began selling succulent arrangements and plants almost two decades ago. Her award-winning succulent garlands and displays have been featured at world-famous hotels, botanical gardens, an internationally known theme park, and tourist attractions. Her work has appeared in *House Beautiful* magazine, *HGTV Magazine*, and *Pioneer Woman* magazine.

Julia had a wedding bouquet featured in a prime-time drama on FOX TV. Her wedding creations have also been featured in *Style Me Pretty Weddings* magazine and The Knot.

yellow pear ◯ press

Yellow Pear Press, established in 2015, publishes inspiring, charming, clever, distinctive, playful, imaginative, beautifully designed lifestyle books, cookbooks, literary fiction, notecards, and journals with a certain *joie de vivre* in both content and style. Yellow Pear Press books have been honored by the Independent Publisher Book (IPPY) Awards, National Indie Excellence Awards, Independent Press Awards, and International Book Awards. Reviews of our titles have appeared in Kirkus Reviews, Foreword Reviews, Booklist, Midwest Book Review, San Francisco Chronicle, and New York Journal of Books, among others. Yellow Pear Press joined forces with Mango Publishing in 2020, with the vision to continue publishing clever and innovative books. The fact that they're both named after fruit is a total coincidence.

We love hearing from our readers, so please stay in touch with us and follow us at:

Facebook: Mango Publishing
Twitter: @MangoPublishing
Instagram: @MangoPublishing
LinkedIn: Mango Publishing
Pinterest: Mango Publishing
Newsletter: mangopublishinggroup.com/newsletter

CPSIA information can be obtained
at www.ICGtesting.com
Printed in the USA
JSHW012100150622
27151JS00003B/4